SpringerBriefs in Computer Science

SpringerBriefs present concise summaries of cutting-edge research and practical applications across a wide spectrum of fields. Featuring compact volumes of 50 to 125 pages, the series covers a range of content from professional to academic.

Typical topics might include:

- A timely report of state-of-the art analytical techniques
- A bridge between new research results, as published in journal articles, and a contextual literature review
- A snapshot of a hot or emerging topic
- An in-depth case study or clinical example
- A presentation of core concepts that students must understand in order to make independent contributions

Briefs allow authors to present their ideas and readers to absorb them with minimal time investment. Briefs will be published as part of Springer's eBook collection, with millions of users worldwide. In addition, Briefs will be available for individual print and electronic purchase. Briefs are characterized by fast, global electronic dissemination, standard publishing contracts, easy-to-use manuscript preparation and formatting guidelines, and expedited production schedules. We aim for publication 8–12 weeks after acceptance. Both solicited and unsolicited manuscripts are considered for publication in this series.

**Indexing: This series is indexed in Scopus, Ei-Compendex, and zbMATH **

More information about this series at https://link.springer.com/bookseries/10028

Marwan Omar

Defending Cyber Systems through Reverse Engineering of Criminal Malware

 Springer

Marwan Omar
Illinois Institute of Technology
Chicago, USA

ISSN 2191-5768   ISSN 2191-5776   (electronic)
SpringerBriefs in Computer Science
ISBN 978-3-031-11625-4   ISBN 978-3-031-11626-1   (eBook)
https://doi.org/10.1007/978-3-031-11626-1

This Springer imprint is published by the registered company Springer Nature Switzerland AG
The registered company address is: Gewerbestrasse 11, 6330 Cham, Switzerland

This book is dedicated to my wife, Maha, for inspiring me to write it and for supporting me throughout this journey. Without her unwavering support, this project would not have seen the light of day!

Contents

Chapter 1
Introduction to the Fascinating World of Malware Analysis

Information technology has forever changed the way we live and work, and there is no doubt about the fact that the world has benefited from technological advancements in ways that are immeasurable and never imagined before. However, these technological advancements are not risk-free, and there is a flip side to this: cyber-criminal activities have skyrocketed in the recent years to the point where in some cases hackers have been able to take business organization as hostage using malware.

Most cyber-attacks involve deploying some type of malware. Malware that viciously targets every industry, every sector, every enterprise, and even individuals has shown its capabilities to take the entire business organizations offline and cause significant financial damage in billions of dollars annually. Malware authors are constantly evolving in their attack strategies and sophistication and are developing malware that is difficult to detect and can lay dormant in the background for quite some time in order to evade security controls.

Our cyber space is quickly becoming over-whelmed with ever-evolving malware that breaches all security defenses, works viciously in the background without user awareness or interaction, and secretly leaks confidential business data. In order to stop hackers in their tracks and beat cybercriminals in their own game, we need to equip cyber security professionals with the knowledge and skills necessary to detect and respond to malware attacks. Learning and mastering the inner workings of malware will help in the fight against the ever-changing malware landscape. This learning is pursued via malware analysis techniques which could be performed statically, automatically, dynamically, or on the code level.

M. Omar, *Defending Cyber Systems through Reverse Engineering of Criminal Malware*, SpringerBriefs in Computer Science, https://doi.org/10.1007/978-3-031-11626-1_1

What Is Malware Analysis?

Before we try to understand what malware analysis is and why malware analysis is important in the context of cyber security, let's try to define malware. Malware is code that is utilized to perform malicious actions with the intent of causing harm and destruction on computer system and networks. Malware is typically designed to take advantage of some type of security flaw or backdoor and benefit at the victim's expense. Moreover, malware is often written by people or organizations to use its capabilities for malicious intentions and purpose.

Malware analysis aims to examine malware's behavior. The objective of malware analysis is to gain an understanding of the inner workings of malware and how to detect and remove it. To reliably analyze malware, we analyze the malware specimen in a safe environment to identify its characteristics and functionalities so security defenses can be developed to secure and protect a business organization's digital assets (Monnappa, 2018).

Many of the cyber incidents and data breaches that we see and hear about in the news are typically carried out using some sort of malware, which might be designed to enable the attacker to gain remote control of a compromised computing system, steal business sensitive data, spy on the victim's online activities, spread within the victim/target organization, and so on. That's where the importance of knowing how to examine and analyze malicious program comes into play as it's critical to be able to control the situation and minimize the damage and disruption to business operations and the organization at large (Afianian et al., 2020).

One of the most pressing challenges faced by business organizations when they experience a cyber-attack is that, more often than not, those organizations do not have the knowledge nor readiness of how to analyze malware once it has been discovered on their production computer networks. This is where this book can help; this book brief will help shed some light on the tools and techniques needed to properly analyze malicious programs to determine their characteristics which can prove extremely helpful when investigating data breaches as those tools and techniques will provide insights to incident response teams and digital investigation professionals. Some of the key things that cyber professionals can learn when analyzing malware are questions related to the nature of threat posed by malware; the objective of the adversary using the malware; how to contain, eradicate, and recover from an incident; and perhaps more importantly, how to strengthen cyber defenses so that the cyber-attack does not reoccur in the future (Monnappa, 2018).

Malware Analysis Techniques

The process of analyzing malware should be a methodical one and generally involves several stages, which can be viewed in the order of increasing complexity. The pyramid below has been used to illustrate such one ranking:

Fig. 1.1 Malware analysis techniques

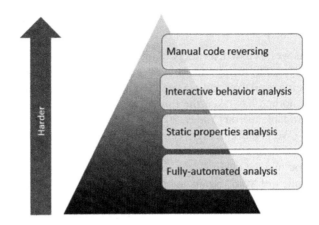

Fully automated tools can offer an easy and simple way to examine and analyze a particular malware specimen (as shown in the figure above, Fig. 1.1), some of which are available as commercial products and some as free ones. These tools are designed as a triage method to quickly assess the behavior of the specimen if it ran on a system. They typically produce reports with details such as the registry keys used by the malicious program, network traffic, and so on. The down side of those fully automated utilities is that they may not provide as much insight as human analysts would obtain when examining the specimen in a more manual manner. On the flip side, and as a benefit, they can contribute to the incident response by rapidly handling vast amounts of malware, allowing malware examiners to focus on the malicious binaries that truly require their time and attention (Han et al., 2014).

Lab Setup for Detecting, Dissecting, and Analyzing Malware

Analysis of a hostile program requires a safe and secure lab environment, as you do not want to infect your system or the production system. A malware lab can be very simple or complex depending on the resources available to you (hardware, virtualization software, Windows license, and so on). This section will guide you to set up a simple personal lab on a single physical system consisting of virtual machines (VMs).

To effectively and safely analyze malicious software, we need to ensure that we have a laboratory environment that can accommodate key malware analysis phases; after all we do not want to infect our personal machines or the production environment. This entails isolating the lab from other networks, installing the appropriate tools, and confirming that the overall configuration of the laboratory environment can accommodate our analysis objectives.

Lab Requirements

As we discussed, a variety of information sources on the Internet can provide details relevant to the specimen we need to analyze. However, we cannot count on them being available, and we need to know how to examine the malicious program even if no one has taken the time to perform the analysis earlier or made the findings available to you (Yadav, 2019).

We could employ free and commercial tools outside of our environment that shed details on various aspects of the malicious program. However, in some cases, you may be dealing with a sensitive incident that—due to its nature or the overall policy of your organization—precludes you from sending the sample outside of your environment. All this is to say that you need to have tools of your own to analyze malicious programs so that you can go beyond the details what third-party tools or information sources can offer. You need a lab.

The lab should be isolated from other networks. Such isolation mitigates the risk of malware escaping from your lab to infect production systems. It also helps prevent situations in which the analyst might inadvertently infect the wrong system. Isolating the lab also makes it less likely that the malware you examine accidentally attacks other people or organizations (Afianian et al., 2020).

Finally, isolating the lab gives you the degree of control over its configuration that's needed to examine malware in a reliable and repeatable manner. If the lab were connected to other networks, you would have a harder time controlling what IT resources are available to the specimen and how it interacts with its environment. Your lab should have the tools you know and trust to examine malware using behavioral and code analysis techniques. You get to know many such tools throughout the book, perhaps to enhance the toolkit you already have or to give you the opportunity to experiment with new tools and approaches. The malware analysis lab should incorporate several systems networked together.

Since modern malware tends to behave and operate differently under different circumstances, it would not hurt to consider including both older operating systems (e.g., Windows 7) and more modern ones (e.g., Windows 10). You might also benefit from having a Linux host in the lab, even if you don't examine Linux-based malware. Many tools that can help examine Windows-centric malware run on Linux. A Linux host is also useful for running or emulating the various network services that malware might want to access when it runs.

The screen capture above (Fig. 1.2) shows an example of a simple lab architecture. The network addressing scheme and specific systems present in your lab might differ from what you see on this screen capture. Such a lab could be implemented using physically distinct components or using virtualization.

Building a lab architecture using virtualization software is highly appreciated by malware analysts due to the flexibility and convenience offered by virtualization products. Such tools enable multiple virtual systems, sometimes called guests or virtual machines (VMS), to run on a single physical host. The virtualization tool

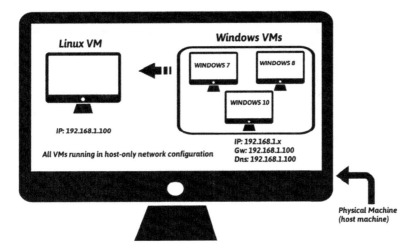

Fig. 1.2 Lab setup diagram

emulates (or "virtualizes") the hardware for each VM. You still need to install the operating system and applications into the VMS, much like you would install them onto a traditional physical host. Virtualization software emulates (or "virtualizes") the network within the host, allowing the VMS to interact with each other as if they were plugged into the physical network. You have a lot of control over the virtualized network's configuration, so you can define how the virtualized network is structured and how and whether it can communicate with the physical network (Monnappa, 2018).

Virtualization software includes such products as VMware Workstation, Microsoft Hyper-V, and Oracle VirtualBox. This book uses VMware Workstation or Fusion products. We're sticking with VMware mostly because of that tool's maturity. We already touched on the need to isolate your lab, but it's worth emphasizing this point again due to its importance, especially if you virtualize the lab. Malicious software might look for bugs or configuration weaknesses to escape from one VM to another or onto your physical host. Perhaps more likely, you might accidentally infect the wrong system when experimenting with malware.

Risks Associated with Analyzing Malware

Analyzing malware presents risks and challenges because there is always the possibility of infecting personal systems or production environments when running a hostile program. Fortunately, there are steps you can take to minimize the risk associated with malware analysis to an acceptable level. First, we need to isolate our lab as discussed earlier and void connecting the lab's network to other networks.

Second, if are using virtualization, don't use the lab's physical host for other purposes. Third, it's vital to install the latest security patches, updates, and hotfixes on your virtualization software, the operating system of your physical host, and the tools you use for examining malware. Finally, to further minimize the attack surface of the laboratory environment, disable risky capabilities related to your virtualization software. For instance, consider disabling folder sharing that VMware support to make it less likely that malware can break out of the VM. To further reduce the risk, consider avoiding the use of VMware tools altogether (Monnappa, 2018).

When mentioning virtualization, it's worth stating that some malware includes "self-defending" capabilities to detect whether it's being analyzed. This capability might entail the use of virtualization and spotting other malware analysis utilities that are part of your toolkit. Such approaches make it harder for automated tools to spot the specimen. They also make it harder for malware analysts to examine its functionality. If malware believes it's being analyzed, it may try to terminate the offending tools, refuse to run, or from how it would in a non-laboratory system.

There are several ways to deal with malware that detects the presence of our analysis tools. For instance, you can use a dedicated physical system for performing your analysis instead of using a virtualization tool.

When preparing your lab, consider how you can save and restore the state of your system before you infect it. After all, you wouldn't want to install the operating system and your tools from scratch at the end of your experiment. Virtualization software provides a convenient mechanism for doing this. Such software enables you to take an almost instantaneous snapshot of the virtual machine, and it gives you the ability to revert to that snapshot almost as quickly (Monnappa, 2018).

You'll probably want to take a snapshot of your VM while it's still clean. In addition, you might take snapshots periodically as you progress through the analysis process, in case you'd like to repeat some of your steps without having to start from the beginning. Conveniently, VMware Workstation and Fusion enable analysts to take multiple snapshots of the VM. Snapshots also help maintain different noninfected versions of the VM. For instance, you might periodically apply security patches to your laboratory systems. Snapshots of the various patch levels enable you to experiment with malware in different environments, which is especially useful for examining malicious programs that exploit known vulnerabilities (Bat-Erdene et al., 2017).

We'll use a very methodical approach along with many handy tools throughout this book to examine malicious software. They can be used for performing tasks related to static properties analysis, behavioral analysis, and code analysis of malware.

References

Afianian, A., Niksefat, S., Sadeghiyan, B., & Baptiste, D. (2020). Malware dynamic analysis evasion techniques: A survey. *ACM Computing Surveys, 52*(6), 1–28. https://doi.org/10.1145/3365001

Bat-Erdene, M., Park, H., Li, H., Lee, H., & Choi, M.-S. (2017). Entropy analysis to classify unknown packing algorithms for malware detection. *International Journal of Information Security, 16*(3), 227–248. https://doi.org/10.1007/s10207-016-0330-4

Han, X. G., Qu, W., Yao, X. X., Guo, C. Y., & Zhou, F. (2014). Research on malicious code variants detection based on texture fingerprint. *Journal on Communications, 35*(8), 125–136.

Monnappa, K. A. (2018). *Learning malware analysis: Explore the concepts, tools, and techniques to analyze and investigate windows malware.* Packt Publishing. https://www.packtpub.com/product/learning-malware-analysis/9781788392501

Yadav, R. M. (2019). Effective analysis of malware detection in cloud computing. *Computers & Security, 83*, 14–21. https://doi.org/10.1016/j.cose.2018.12.005

Chapter 2
Static Analysis of Malware

Static Analysis

Static analysis is one of the malware analysis techniques used by malware analysts to quickly triage suspect programs/files without executing them. During this initial assessment phase, the goal is to be able to extract valuable insights from the suspect binary which would help inform the subsequent steps so that we can determine how to analyze or categorize the suspect file and where to focus our analysis efforts (Kirubavathi & Anitha, 2018).

This chapter covers various tools and techniques to extract valuable information from the suspect binary. In this chapter, you will learn the following: identifying the malware's target architecture; fingerprinting the malware; scanning the suspect binary with anti-virus engines; extracting strings, functions, and metadata associated with the file; identifying the obfuscation techniques used to thwart analysis; and classifying and comparing the malware samples.

These techniques can reveal different information about the file. It is not required to follow all these techniques, and they need not be followed in the order presented. The choice of techniques to use depends on your goal and the context surrounding the suspect file.

Static properties analysis examines the static properties of suspicious files such as file hashes, embedded resources, digital certificates, and interesting strings. A good starting point to analyzing potential malware files is the static properties analysis. The objective of the static properties analysis is to quickly assess the nature of a potential malware file and develop plans for taking a closer look in the subsequent phases of malware analysis (Sibi Chakkaravarthy et al., 2019).

The best way to demonstrate how to apply the static analysis technique is to use a real-world malware sample that exhibits static properties. We will consider a fictional enterprise security incident scenario whereby a system is misbehaving and showing indicators of compromise (IOCs). The said system is suddenly rebooting

M. Omar, *Defending Cyber Systems through Reverse Engineering of Criminal Malware*, SpringerBriefs in Computer Science, https://doi.org/10.1007/978-3-031-11626-1_2

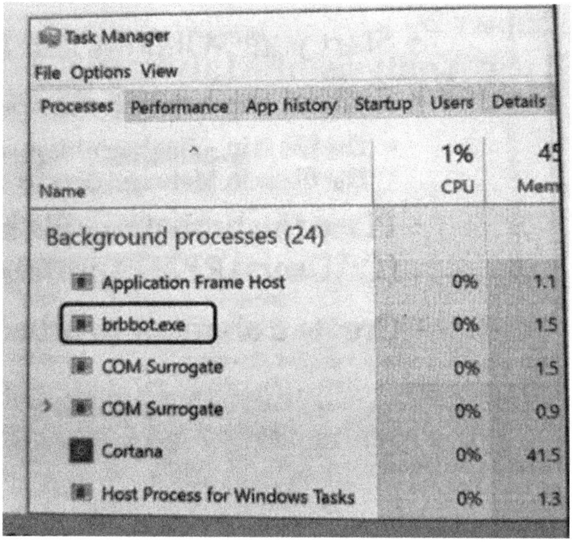

Fig. 2.1 Foreign process running on the system

and is experiencing slow performance; in addition, there is a foreign process called brbbot.exe (Fig. 2.1) running from %AppData%.

The %AppData% is an environment variable on Windows that typically points to a directory in the user's profile, such as C:\Users\REM\AppData\Roaming. This location is designed for storing "user-specific files that applications install" according to Microsoft. Technet.microsoft.com.

As a "rule of thumb," when we run malware in our lab, we want to determine what is the worst that the malware specimen can do, giving it the opportunity to reach its full malicious potential. That said, we will make the brbbot specimen run in the virtual lab system and infect our virtual host with this potential malware, all of this is done with full administrator privileges to allow the potential malware sample to exhibit its full malicious potential, as mentioned earlier.

This approach will help us in making sure that the specimen is able to interact with all aspects of the infected host, allowing it to achieve its full malicious potential. However, sometimes it's also useful to run the specimen with normal, non-administrative privileges to observe its behavior—for instance, if mimicking a particular scenario of a production system in a business setting (Stiborek et al., 2018).

Initial Assessment of a Potential Malware Specimen: brbbot.exe

Prior to deciding whether to examine the malicious (or suspicious) program using behavioral or code analysis techniques, we should consider performing an initial assessment of the malicious binary by examining its static properties (Kara, 2019).

In some cases, the binary may turn out to be not malicious because it possesses a hash that belongs to a trusted program. Performing static properties analysis is important as it can help us determine where to focus our subsequent analysis efforts. Static properties analysis is a useful first step as part of the triage effort.

Given our brbbot.exe specimen, which is a Windows executable, static properties of a Windows executable include asking the following questions:

1. Is it malware?
2. What type of file is it (e.g., .exe, .dll, .com, .sys, and so on)?
3. What is the target architecture (32-bit or 64-bit platform)?
4. How bad is it?
5. How to detect it?
6. How to analyze it?

Some of those properties will be examined using the brbbot.exe sample.

Extracting String

A string can be defined as a sequence of ASCII and Unicode-printable characters embedded within a file. Extracting and examining strings can give malware analysts insights about the program functionality and capabilities. Therefore, a common first step in examining a suspicious file involves looking at the strings imbedded in it. This examination may reveal filenames, domain names, URLs, IP addresses, hostnames, or registry keys that the program may attempt to access and can help focus subsequent steps of the investigation. It must be noted, however, that we cannot trust all the strings embedded into the program because they might have been embedded there to mislead the malware analyst. Not to mention the fact that relying on strings alone does not paint a clear or compelling picture of the purpose and functionality of a malware binary (Carrillo-Mondejar et al., 2020).

A convenient way to accomplish this is to use the pestr tool on REMnux; this utility designed for extracting strings from Windows executable files automatically obtains both ASCII and Unicode-encoded strings in one shot. Alternatively, we could use the well-known "Strings" tool, present on most Linux distributions. By default, *Strings* extracts only ASCI-encoded strings. We can tell the tool to extract Unicode strings by specifying the –encoding=l (lower case L) parameter as shown on the screen capture below (Fig. 2.2).

Another way to examine ASCII and Unicode-encoded strings on a file is to use the GUI tool BinText, available free from http://www.mcafee.com/us/downloads/free-tools/bintext.aspx. BinText's Filter tab (Fig. 2.3) enables you to configure parameters such as what characters the tool considers as belonging to a string, as well as the minimum number of characters the tool considers as belonging to a string. The default minimum text length value is 5. You can decrease it to find shorter strings.

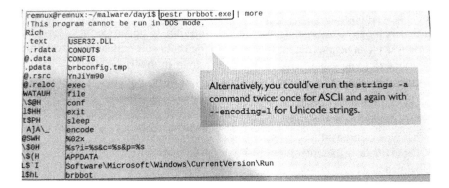

Fig. 2.2 Pestr string helps extract strings from a malicious executable

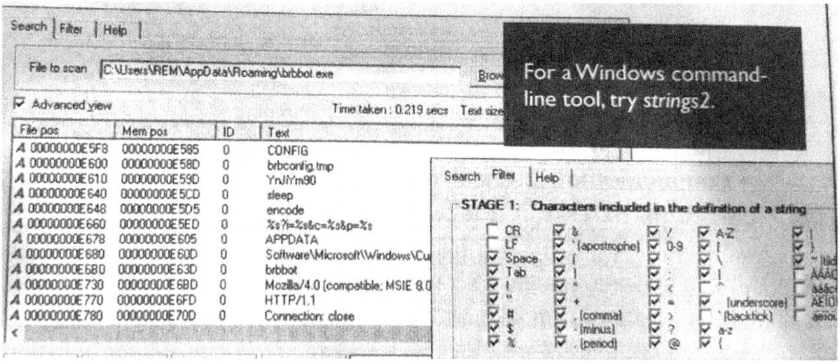

Fig. 2.3 Bin Text as a GUI to examine embedded strings on Windows

Strings Embedded in brbbot.exe Suggest a Few Potential Characteristics

By examining the strings embedded inside brbbot.exe, we can probably begin developing some hypothesis about its characteristics. For instance, the string HTTP/I.1 might imply that this program can communicate over HTTP. The string referring to the ... Run registry key suggests that this program might use this key as a persistence mechanism.

Strings might also enable us to formulate indicators of compromise (IOCs), which can help in identifying systems throughout our organization infected with this specimen. Potential IOCs based on strings are the brbbconfig.tmp file and the string %s?i=%s&c=%s&p=%s as part of an HTTP request. Along these lines, the string that began with Mozi1a 1/4.0 could be a specific User-Agent header sent as part of the specimen's HTTP request; this could help us spot the associated network traffic in our environment (Feizollah et al., 2017).

Thus far, we have assumptions and theories, which have not been validated yet. To verify and validate the above theories, we will need to take our efforts to the next level and perform behavioral and code analysis. In most cases, conducting static analysis on a suspect binary is a necessary and important first step to inform the next steps (behavioral and code analysis) of the malware analysis process.

Deep-Dive into Static Properties Analysis Using PeStudio

In addition to the embedded strings, many other static properties are worth examining at the onset of the malware analysis process. PeStudio is a handy, free Windows tool that can display both ASCII and Unicode strings. PeStudio is an amazing portable executable analysis tool for assisting with the triage of a malicious program and is designed to retrieve and display various attributes from a portable executable (PE) header, as you can see on the screenshot below. The free version of this tool can be downloaded from https://www.winitor.com.

Among many details about the specimen, PeStudio calculates various hash values. You can use such values as unique identifiers of the file you're examining. Moreover, you can look up these hashes in public and private information sources to obtain additional data about the malicious program you're examining. For the purpose of this walkthrough, we won't perform such lookups so that we learn to handle situations where no third-party details are available to us (Xue et al., 2019).

The following screen capture (Fig. 2.4) displays some of the *ASCII* and *Unicode* strings in PeStudio; this is helpful because it highlights some of the most interesting strings in the suspect binary using the blacklisted column.

One of the most useful features of PeStudio is its Indicators area, which automatically highlights potentially malicious aspects of the Windows executable that the tool is examining. You can see the characteristics that PeStudio considers suspicious for brbbot.exe by clicking the Indicators area of the tool.

You can tweak which aspects of files PeStudio considers "blacklisted" and other aspects of the tool's functionality by editing the XML configuration files that reside under the folder where the tool is installed (e.g., C:\Program Files (x86)\PeStudio\xml). PeStudio offers malware analysts a convenient way of examining many useful

		type	size	loca...	blacklisted (61)	item (372)
c:\users\test\desktop\multi.exe						
indicators (3/9)		unicode	7	-	x	AppData
virustotal (n/a)		unicode	45	-	x	Software\Microsoft\Windows\CurrentVersion\Run
dos-stub (64 bytes)		unicode	38	-	x	netsh firewall delete allowedprogram "
file-header (20 bytes)		unicode	4	-	x	.exe
optional-header (224 bytes)		unicode	30	-	x	cmd.exe /c ping 0 -n 2 & del "
directories (5/15)		unicode	35	-	x	netsh firewall add allowedprogram "
sections (3)		unicode	13	-	x	Execute ERROR
libraries (1)		unicode	14	-	x	Download ERROR
imports (1)		unicode	5	-	x	start
exports (n/a)		unicode	12	-	x	Update ERROR
exceptions (n/a)		unicode	7	-	x	[ENTER]
tls-callbacks (n/a)		ascii	40	-	-	!This program cannot be run in DOS mode.
resources (1)		ascii	5	-	-	.text
strings (61/372)		ascii	7	-	-	@.reloc
debug (n/a)		ascii	4	-	-	3)r]
manifest (invoker)						

Fig. 2.4 Screen capture of PeStudio showing embedded strings in brbbot.exe

properties of a suspicious Windows executable statically, helping you formulate the path for subsequent analysis steps. It's well suited for the triage process (Lim & Yi, 2016).

As illustrated on the screen capture above, PeStudio shows hashes of the file that it is examining. These hashes can be used to fingerprint the malware binary which could then become part of the malware analysis findings.

Additionally, hash values could be used as indicators of compromise (IOCs), enabling malware analysts to detect the malicious file regardless of its filename. However, malware authors can easily tweak the specimen to change the file's hash without changing the specimen's functionality. For this reason, it's also useful to note hash values of the sections that comprise the malicious program, which PeStudio computes as well. This way, if the attacker changes a portion of the file, hash values of one or more sections might still match as an IOC (Carlin et al., 2019).

It's worth noting that Windows executable files with sections are those types of files that typically contain several groupings of code and data, organized into sections. PeStudio shows that brbbot.exe is composed of several sections: .text, data, .rsrc, and .reloc.

More Details of brbbot.exe from PeStudio

Among other details, PeStudio also displays contents of the specimen's import table in the area labeled "imports." Windows uses this information to determine which DLLs ("libraries") and the functions implemented within them ("symbols" or "APIs") are necessary for the program's execution. Looking at imports can help us determine the type of functionality implemented within the specimen. For instance, the presence of LoadLibraryW indicates that the specimen can load additional DLLs during runtime. If you scrolled down in the listing of imports, you would see the RegSetValueExA symbol, which suggests that the sample has the capability to set registry values, while seeing CryptDeriveKey indicates the use of Windows cryptographic capabilities.

As you can see, PeStudio presents a wealth of information about the file.

Alternative Tools

For alternatives to PeStudio, we can experiment with peframe (Fig. 2.5) and pescanner.py command-line tools on REMnux. Both utilities extract a wealth of details about the Windows executable using static analysis and bring to your attention the most interesting properties.

You can learn more about peframe by visiting https://github.com/guelfoweb/peframe.

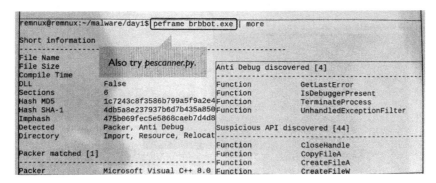

Fig. 2.5 Screen capture showing peframe to extract interesting file properties

As we examine the output of these tools, we should keep in mind that any conclusions we draw from static properties analysis are theories that need to be validated in subsequent analysis steps. For instance, though peframe flags the specimen's use of GetLastError as an anti-debugging technique, it's possible that a call to this function serves another purpose (Ul Haq et al., 2018).

Portable Executable Headers

The portable executable file format is the standard format for dynamic link libraries (DLLs), executables (.exe), and common object files (COC). Files with extensions such as (.exe, .dll, and .sys) are called portable executables. "PE file is a series of structures and sub-components that contain the information required by the operating system to load it into memory" (Monnappa, 2018).

The PE header is considered a wealth of information for malware reverse engineers because it contains information such as where the executable needs to be loaded into memory, the address where the execution starts, the list of libraries/functions on which the application relies on, and the resources used by the binary.

Windows executable files follow the PE (portable executable) format. According to PE specifications, such programs have a specially formatted header that contains the details the operating system needs to load the file into memory and set up the runtime environment for the process so it can run properly. Looking at some aspects of the PE header can be useful for assessing the nature of the specimen (Yadav, 2019).

PeStudio, which we examined a bit earlier, relied on PE header contents when displaying some of the information we found helpful. In addition, consider incorporating into your toolkit the two tools shown in the screen capture below (Fig. 2.6): Detect It Easy (DIE) and Exeinfo PE. These utilities are especially useful for determining which tools were used to generate the executable file you're examining.

Malicious executables tend to be created using the same tools developers use to create legitimate software, such as Visual Studio. Afterward, malware authors might

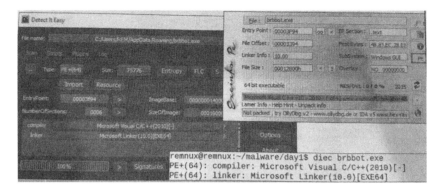

Fig. 2.6 Screenshot showing Detect It Easy and Exeinfo PE shows PE header details

pack their creations to make it harder for us to examine them (Ni et al., 2018). Packing typically involves obfuscating, encrypting, or otherwise encoding the original executable to create a new file that embeds the original program as data. When the packed program runs, it unpacks itself into the memory of the infected host. It can be useful to determine whether the file is packed and, if it is, which packer was used to safeguard the original file. Detect It Easy and Exeinfo PE can help with these tasks. These tools show that brbbot.exe is not packed and was probably created in C or C++ using Visual Studio.

You can download Exeinfo PE from http://www.exeinfo.xn.pl. Exeinfo PE also has the capability to other words, carve—any file, extracting from within the file embedded artifacts.

Summarizing the Static Properties Analysis

Static properties analysis is an important first step to methodically analyze malware; it enables malware analysts to conveniently and quickly glean valuable information and insights from the malicious program which would help with subsequent analysis steps. In this chapter, we learned about various tools and techniques that can be used to learn about different aspects of a malicious binary without executing. We've been examining static properties of a suspicious file (brbbot.exe) to assess the likelihood that it's malicious and to get a sense for what we might encounter if we examined it further using behavioral and code analysis techniques. In the process, we discovered several potential IOCs for this specimen and saw indications of potential functionality related to HTTP communications, registry and file activity, and encryption. These steps have enabled us to formulate theories about the specimen's characteristics, which we will validate in the subsequent analysis steps. In the next chapter, "Behavioral Analysis," we will explore and learn about behavioral analysis of malware by executing it safely and effectively in an isolated and control lab system.

References

Carlin, D., O'Kane, P., & Sezer, S. (2019). A cost analysis of machine learning using dynamic runtime opcodes for malware detection. *Computers & Security, 85*, 138–155. https://doi.org/10.1016/j.cose.2019.04.018

Carrillo-Mondejar, J., Castelo, G. J. M., Nunez-Gomez, C., Roldan, G. J., & Martinez, J. L. (2020). Automatic analysis architecture of iot malware samples. *Security and Communication Networks, 2020.* https://doi.org/10.1155/2020/8810708

Feizollah, A., Anuar, N. B., Salleh, R., Suarez-Tangil, G., & Furnell, S. (2017). Androdialysis: Analysis of android intent effectiveness in malware detection. *Computers & Security, 65*, 121–134. https://doi.org/10.1016/j.cose.2016.11.007

Kara, I. (2019). A basic malware analysis method. *Computer Fraud & Security, 2019*(6), 11–19.

Kirubavathi, G., & Anitha, R. (2018). Structural analysis and detection of android botnets using machine learning techniques. *International Journal of Information Security, 17*(2), 153–167. https://doi.org/10.1007/s10207-017-0363-3

Lim, J., & Yi, J. H. (2016). Structural analysis of packing schemes for extracting hidden codes in mobile malware. *EURASIP Journal on Wireless Communications and Networking, 2016*(1), 1–12. https://doi.org/10.1186/s13638-016-0720-3

Monnappa, K. A. (2018). *Learning malware analysis: Explore the concepts, tools, and techniques to analyze and investigate windows malware.* Packt Publishing. https://www.packtpub.com/product/learning-malware-analysis/9781788392501

Ni, S., Qian, Q., & Zhang, R. (2018). Malware identification using visualization images and deep learning. *Computers & Security, 77*, 871–885. https://doi.org/10.1016/j.cose.2018.04.005

Sibi Chakkaravarthy, S., Sangeetha, D., & Vaidehi, V. (2019). A survey on malware analysis and mitigation techniques. *Computer Science Review, 32*, 1–23. https://doi.org/10.1016/j.cosrev.2019.01.002

Stiborek, J., Pevný, T., & Rehák, M. (2018). Probabilistic analysis of dynamic malware traces. *Computers & Security, 74*, 221–239. https://doi.org/10.1016/j.cose.2018.01.012

Ul Haq, I., Chica, S., Caballero, J., & Jha, S. (2018). Malware lineage in the wild. *Computers & Security, 78*, 347–363. https://doi.org/10.1016/j.cose.2018.07.012

Xue, D., Li, J., Wu, W., Tian, Q., & Wang, J. (2019). Homology analysis of malware based on ensemble learning and multifeatures. *PLoS One, 14*(8), 0211373. https://doi.org/10.1371/journal.pone.0211373

Yadav, R. M. (2019). Effective analysis of malware detection in cloud computing. *Computers & Security, 83*, 14–21. https://doi.org/10.1016/j.cose.2018.12.005

Chapter 3
Behavioral Analysis Principles

Behavioral Analysis Principles

Behavioral (also referred to as dynamic analysis) entails analyzing a specimen by triggering it to run in an isolated and controlled lab environment and monitoring its behavior, interaction, and impact on the system. In the previous chapter, we learned the techniques, tools, and principles to examine the different aspects of the suspect specimen without executing it. In this chapter, we will capitalize on that knowledge to further observe the behavior, purpose, and functionality of the suspect specimen using dynamic analysis. You will learn the behavioral analysis tools and their features and simulate Internet services. Our goal during this analysis phase is to observe and monitor malware behavior and better understand its characteristics (Ul Haq et al., 2018).

We are now ready to take a closer look at brbbot.exe by observing how it behaves when it runs within our lab. In the process, we will learn several practical malware analysis techniques that you'll be able to apply to other samples that may be encountered in real-life contexts.

Behavioral Analysis Tools

Prior to conducting the behavioral analysis technique, it is critical to understand the tools that you will utilize to monitor the specimen's behavior. In this chapter, you will learn about various behavioral malware analysis tools. If you have set up your lab environment as described in Chap. 1, you can download these tools to your host machine and then install those tools to your virtual machines and take a new, clean snapshot. We will cover a few behavioral analysis tools and their core features. We

M. Omar, *Defending Cyber Systems through Reverse Engineering of Criminal Malware*, SpringerBriefs in Computer Science,
https://doi.org/10.1007/978-3-031-11626-1_3

will also learn how to use these tools to monitor the behavior of the malware in a controlled environment and in real time.

Process Hacker

Process Hacker is an open-source, multi-purpose tool designed to help analysts monitor system resources, processes running, networking activity, and detect malware (Afianian et al., 2020). It is a powerful replacement for the Task Manager built into Windows. The capabilities of Process Hacker are similar to those of a free tool that you can download from Microsoft, called Process Explorer. (See https://technet.microsoft.com/en-us/sysinternals/processexplorer.aspx.)

Another powerful component of our toolkit is Process Monitor. It's available free from Microsoft at https://technet.microsoft.com/en-us/sysinternals/bb896645.aspx. This tool "shows real-time file system, registry, and activity" of processes on the infected Windows laboratory system, recording all observed actions in a detailed log file. We will also use a companion tool, ProcDOT, to examine key aspects of the Process Monitor log in a convenient manner. ProcDOT is available free from http://www.procdot.com. The following screenshot (Fig. 3.1) illustrates the various process activities captured by Process Monitor on a pristine system.

We will supplement Process Monitor's insights with a report from Regshot. This open-source tool enables analysts to determine how the malicious program changed the state of the file system and the registry of its host during the infection. To accomplish this, we will use Regshot to compare the state of the system before and after the infection and examine the report that the tool generates to highlight the changes. Regshot is available at https://sourceforge.net/projects/regshot.

Wireshark is a popular open-source network sniffer, available at https://www.wireshark.org. It will give us excellent visibility into the laboratory's network traffic associated with the specimen.

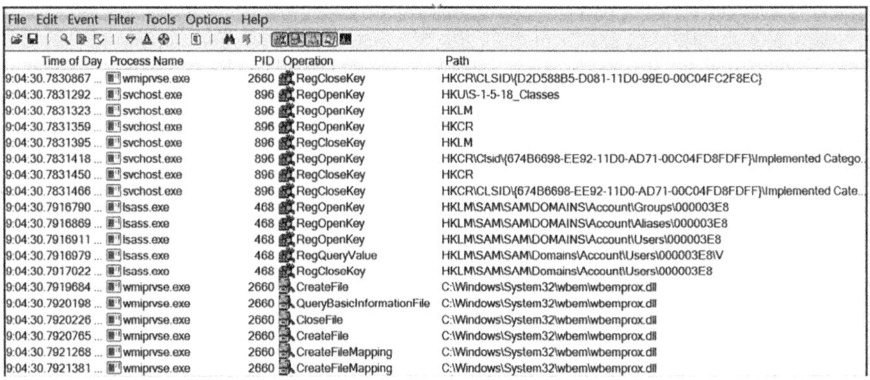

Fig. 3.1 Screenshot of Process Monitor shows how it displays information about running processes and events

Process Hacker's Network tab shows only the connections active at a given moment. What if a specimen performed a network action so quickly that you didn't spot it in Process Hacker's Network tab? Wireshark maintains a historical record, but it doesn't specify which local process was involved in the connection. At this point, TcpLogView can help. This free tool, available from http://www.nirsoft.net/utils/tcp_log_view.html, "monitors the opened TCP connections on your system, and adds a new log line every time that a TCP connection is opened or closed."

Conducting Behavioral Analysis Using brbbot.exe

Before infecting the lab system, we will launch a few monitoring tools. We will start by running Process Hacker on the virtual machine. Familiarize yourself with the process listing, services, and network connections on the system while it is still clean. You'll use Process Hacker to spot the malicious process after infecting the system and, if possible, to terminate that process when you no longer need it (Zhang & Song, 2020).

The listing of processes on your VM will look similar to what's captured on the screen capture below (Fig. 3.2), though it might not match the screenshot exactly.

Spend a few minutes getting to know the user interface of this tool. For example, you can right-click a process that interests you, select properties, and examine and even edit its runtime memory. We won't cover all the features built into Process Hacker that might be useful to a malware analyst, but we will discuss the most important ones.

Note that Process Hacker shows the parent-child relationship of the active processes. For each process, it displays details such as its name and process identifier (PID), whether address space layout randomization (ASLR) is enabled for it, and what its integrity level is.

Next, we will run Process Monitor (Fig. 3.3) in Windows REM Workstation. This tool will enable us to record a log of the specimen's system, registry, and some

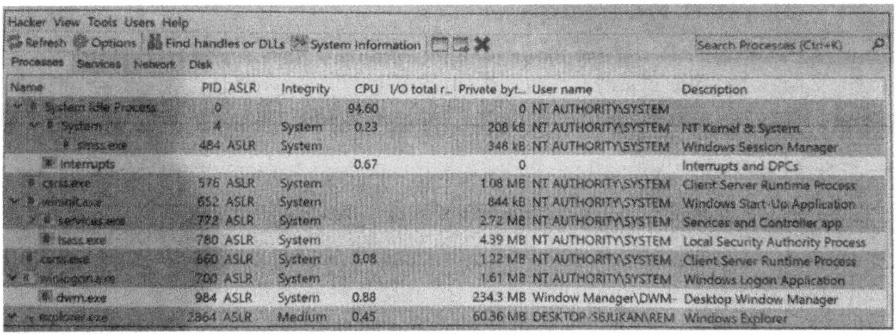

Fig. 3.2 Screen capture of Process Hacker shows a list of applications and processes running on the system

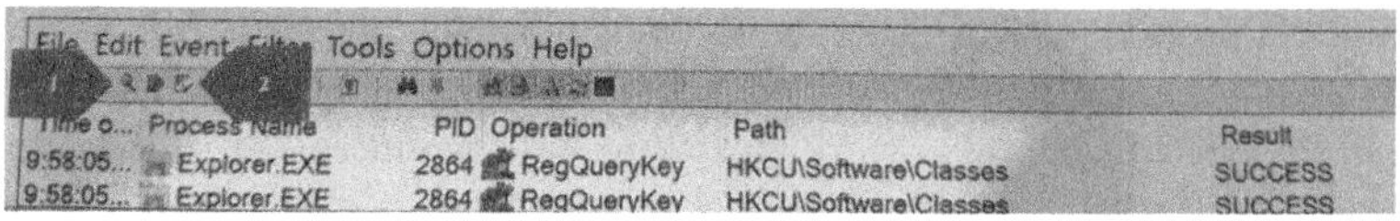

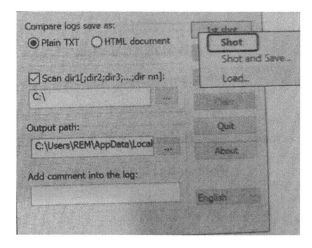

Fig. 3.3 A screenshot showing a Process Monitor interface and the list of events

Fig. 3.4 A screenshot showing how to take the first snapshot using Regshot

network-related operations. As soon as Process Monitor launches, it begins recording the activities of currently running processes. You see activities that are a part of the normal operation of Windows: files being accessed and registry keys being queried and sometimes set.

To keep the amount of noise in the Process Monitor log to a minimum, press Ctrl+E (or click the button that looks like a magnifying glass) in Process Monitor to pause capture until you are ready to infect the system. After pausing the capture, press Ctrl+X (or click the button that looks like an eraser floating over a sheet of paper) to clear the log. You will begin Process Monitor's capture immediately before infecting the system, but we're not ready to do that yet.

We will minimize Process Hacker and Process Monitor for now, so it's easier to focus on the next set of tools we launch.

Regshot

You can use Regshot during behavioral analysis to create a baseline of the pristine system and compare it to the system's state after the malicious program ran. Using Regshot with tools such as Process Monitor enables us to be relatively certain that we can observe the specimen's effect on the infected system.

After launching Regshot, click the first shot button, and then click Shot to take the snapshot of your Windows REM Workstation's file system and registry while the VM is still clean (Fig. 3.4). When taking the snapshot, Regshot computes checksums of all files and registry keys, so it can later spot which of these objects have changed.

After taking the first snapshot using Regshot, minimize the tool. You will take the second snapshot a bit later after you've infected the system with brbbot.exe.

Wireshark for Capturing Network Traffic

To understand how a suspect binary interacts with its environment and what communication paths it uses, it will be necessary to sniff and capture network traffic to determine network-based indicators of compromise (IOCs). One of the best tools to assist with this task is Wireshark which is an open-source, powerful network protocol sniffer that enables you to monitor and capture network communications.

Now, we will switch to REMnux virtual machine and type wireshark & at the terminal prompt to launch Wireshark. We'll use this sniffer to monitor the laboratory network while infecting the Windows virtual machine with brbbot.exe.

In general, it's good to run monitoring tools on a system other than the one you're infecting. This way, the specimen is less likely to detect that it's being observed or to interfere with the monitoring tools. The utilities we have launched in preparation for infecting the system so far have to execute on the system where the specimen will run. In contrast, a sniffer can be effective on any host within your laboratory network, assuming it operates in a promiscuous mode.

Activate capture in Wireshark by clicking the eth0 line highlighted in the screenshot on the right side of the screen capture below (Fig. 3.5) or by pressing Ctrl+E.

We will leave Wireshark active and go back to your Windows REM Workstation virtual machine.

We're now almost ready to infect your Windows REM Workstation. It's time to re-enable Process Monitor on it. First, make sure you have the brbbot shortcut,

Fig. 3.5 Wireshark interface

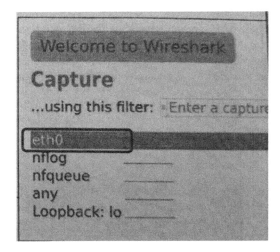

which you created earlier, visible on your screen, so it's easy for you to launch the malicious executable when you're ready to do so. Also, confirm that Process Hacker is running and visible so that you can see the malicious process after you infect the system.

Next, we will activate capture in Process Monitor by clicking the magnifying glass button or pressing Ctrl+E. We will double-click the sh01tcut to brbbot.exe to infect your Windows REM Workstation! When preparing for this step, you modified the shortcut's properties to launch the specimen with full admin rights, giving it the opportunity to show us its full malicious capabilities.

If you look at Process Hacker, you should notice the malicious process running on the now-infected system called brbbot.exe. After letting the process run for about one-half a minute, terminate it using Process Hacker. To do this, right-click the running brbbot.exe process (Fig. 3.6), and select Terminate, or press the Del key on your keyboard. When brbbot.exe is no longer running, go to Process Monitor, and pause capture by clicking the magnifying glass button or pressing Ctrl+E.

Next, switch to the REMnux virtual machine, and pause Wireshark's capture by pressing Ctrl+E or selecting Capture > Stop from its menu. We'll examine what these tools recorded shortly.

Dissecting and Analyzing Behavioral Analysis Findings

Before looking at logs of Process Monitor and Wireshark, let's use Regshot to see how the specimen changed the state of the Windows virtual machine during infection.

Go to the Regshot window where you took the initial snapshot, click the second shot button, and select Shot. ms will take the second snapshot of the state of the file system and the registry. When Regshot finishes scanning the infected system, click the Compare button. The program will launch Notepad, showing you results of the comparison.

Spend some time reviewing the Regshot report to spot interesting entries. Keep in mind that it's normal for Windows to change some aspects of its state when it runs. Therefore, the report will show many changes (especially registry ones) that are not directly associated with the behavior of brbbot.exe. As you become more

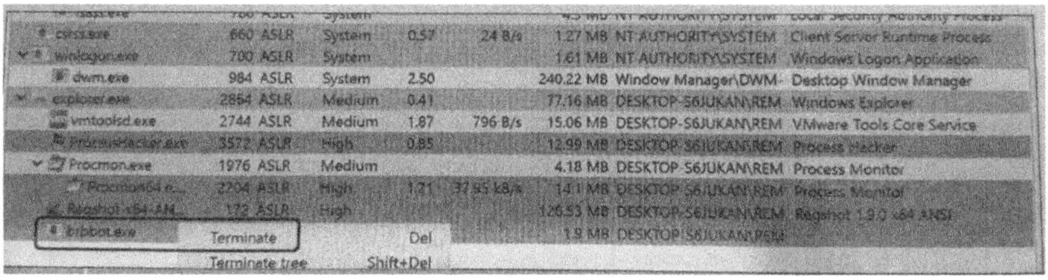

Fig. 3.6 A screenshot showing Process Hacker and brbbot.exe

familiar with looking at the state of your Windows REM Workstation, it will be easier for you to mentally filter out those activities and spot those that might be relevant to your investigation.

Perhaps the most significant findings in the Regshot report include the observation that the infected system now includes the registry key HKLM\SOFTWARE\ Microsoft\Windows\CurrentVersion\Run\brbbot, which points to the brbbot.exe file. As we discussed earlier, defining such an entry causes this program to run automatically when a user logs in. This looks like a persistence mechanism for the specimen.

Another interesting entry in the Regshot report is the addition of the brbconfig. tmp file in the location where the brbbot.exe file is present. You can attempt to view the brbconfig.tmp file with a text editor such as Notepad or Notepad++. Its contents appear to be encoded in a manner that precludes us from deciphering them. Malware authors often try to protect their executables and associated data from malware analysts with the goal of concealing the program's inner workings and slowing us down, and perhaps we've encountered one such defensive measure.

Time permitting, consider the nature of other entries in the Regshot report that interest you. For instance, you might see a reference to the ... \ PendingFileRenameOperations registry key. It contains hex contents that, once converted into ASCII, correspond with the string \??\C:\Users\REM\AppData\ Roaming\brbconfig.tmp. According to Microsoft, this registry key stores "the names of files to be renamed when the system restarts... The system adds this entry to the registry when a user or program tries to rename a file that is in use" (https://technet. microsoft.com/enus/library/cc960241.aspx). However, in our case, the new name of the file appears to be blank, which seems to cause Windows to delete this file upon a reboot.

Other changes that might have caught your attention could be related to files with the .pf extension. These files are automatically generated by Windows to allow the OS to start the process a bit faster the next time it runs. Though their creation is probably not directly related to the behavior of brbbot.exe, their creation or modification offers some visibility into the specific programs that were executed during the period between two Regshot snapshots.

As you just observed, Regshot offers an easy way to identify major changes to the file system and the registry. However, it cannot provide information about the specific sequence of events or detect temporary changes to the system's state that may have occurred while the specimen was running. Nor does it indicate which process is responsible for the changes. These are some of the reasons that we use Process Monitor to gather detailed logs regarding the specimen's actions.

As you can see in the screenshot above (Fig. 3.7), Process Monitor records one event per line, monitoring the activities of all running processes and displaying them in the order in which they occurred. Each line includes details such as the process name and process identifier (PID), the operation, and the path upon which the operation was acting. The tool also records the result of the operation and any pertinent details that clarify the nature of the activity.

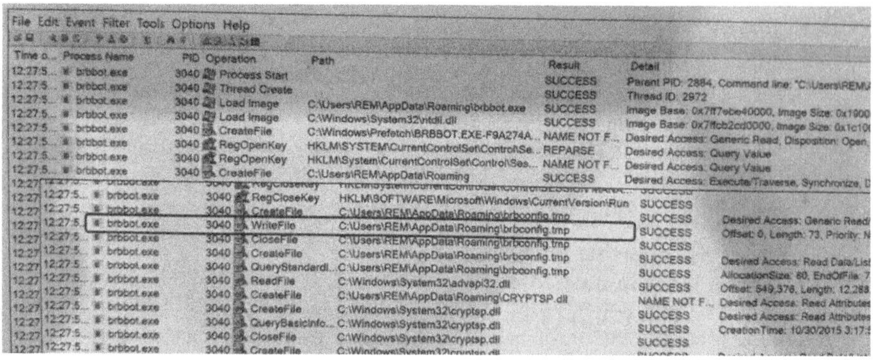

Fig. 3.7 A screenshot showing Process Monitor listing brbbot.exe and the file path

The challenge of spotting interesting events in the Process Monitor is the large amount of data that the tool captures when it runs. Most of those activities are just "noise" generated by legitimate Windows processes and unrelated to the malware specimen. One way to eliminate unwanted entries from view and focus on the entries related to brbbot.exe is to use the filtering capabilities built into Process Monitor. To access this feature, select the Filter menu, and then click on Filter (or press Ctrl+L). You can then define the condition that directs the tool to only display entries where the Process Name is brbbot.exe, as shown on the right side of the screen capture above, and then click OK.

Another way to use Process Monitor's filtering capabilities is to define filters that exclude normal Windows activities, though we won't do that here. This way, you will be able to recall and apply these filters to eliminate lots of records from view that are probably irrelevant to your analysis. You can save such filters by using the Filter > Save Filter menu option. Process Monitor remembers your filters across sessions; however, it won't activate them until you load it using Filter > Load Filter. To see the filters you defined, select Filter > Organize Filters. This window enables you to export custom filters to files with the PMF extension if you want to save the filter for use outside of the lab system. The window also enables you to load PMF files.

After you've defined a filter that only displays the records where the process name is brbbot.exe, spend a few minutes looking through the activities that the process generated when infecting the system.

In the beginning of the Process Monitor log, you see brbbot.exe loading from the file system, its own file in addition to the Windows DLLs it seems to rely on. Numerous registry and file-related actions are not associated with malicious activities but are common to most programs running on the Windows operating system.

With enough scrolling, you can eventually arrive at the events showing the specimen's creation of the brbconfig.tmp file in the C:\Users\REM\AppData\Roaming folder, as captured on the screenshot below. A convenient way to jump to this entry is to press Ctrl+F in Process Monitor and then enter "brbconfig.tmp" and click OK. As you can see, Process Monitor shows us information that corroborates the activities we observed in the Regshot log while providing more details. For instance, we now can reliably say that it was the brbbot.exe process that generated the brbbotconfig.tmp file.

Digging Deeper into the Findings

As you've already seen, we can capture a lot of information about how malicious processes interact with their environment. Process Monitor logs were especially voluminous, filled with useful as well as irrelevant details.

Filtering, navigating, analyzing, and correlating events in Process Monitor can be tricky and time-consuming. Visualizing the relevant details of the logs and identifying relationships between events can help us quickly interpret the data and understand what the malicious program is doing. One way to accomplish this is by using a free tool called ProcDOT, which can correlate, filter, and visualize contents of Process Monitor logs and PCAP network sniffer capture files. ProcDOT is available as a free download from http://www.procdot.com. To see ProcDOT in action, start by exporting the Process Monitor log file in the CSV format. To do this, press Ctrl+S or select File > Save.

Select All events. Select comma-separated values (CSV) as the format. Specify the destination for the file that's easy for you to locate, such as the desktop. To do this, click the. "button (Fig. 3.8) in the Path area of the dialog box, and then navigate to the wanted folder and click OK.

Next, launch ProcDOT on your Windows REM Workstation.

To load your log files into ProcDOT, point ProcDOT to the Process Monitor CSV file by pressing the ". . . " button in the Procmon area. Then click the button in the Launcher area.

ProcDOT will bring up a new window titled "Select the first relevant process." To populate this window's contents, the tool examines the imported Process Monitor log file to determine which processes were active at the time when Process Monitor

Fig. 3.8 A screenshot showing how to load brbbot.exe into ProcDOT

was capturing the data. ProcDOT automatically assigns the light gray color to the processes that were present on the system before Process Monitor began capturing data and presents you with the remaining black-colored process names and IDs. To proceed, double-click the entry that you believe is the first malicious process that started the infection. In our example, that would be brbbot.exe (Fig. 3.9).

Generate the activity diagram by clicking the Refresh button. The next screen capture shows the diagram that ProcDOT will produce as the result. Time permitting, you can later experiment with the "no paths" and "compressed" settings to eliminate additional noise and to simplify the graph. Remember to click Refresh after changing the settings. Note that ProcDOT can also import network sniffer logs in the PCAP format, in which case it can show some network-related details in the generated graph. However, we are not taking advantage of this feature at the moment.

Take a look at the activity graph that ProcDOT generated to illustrate the key brbbot.exe infection events while automatically hiding the irrelevant entries associated with the OS "noise."

ICs easy to spot the persistence-related registry key we observed earlier. ProcDOT labels it as AUTOSTART! You can also see that brbbot.exe creates and then reads the contents of brbconfig.tmp.

There is also an entry related to the specimen creating a file in the …\Microsoft\ Crypto\RSA folder. This entry might appear suspicious at the first glance but is actually a common side effect of a process instantiating a Windows library used for cryptographic operations.

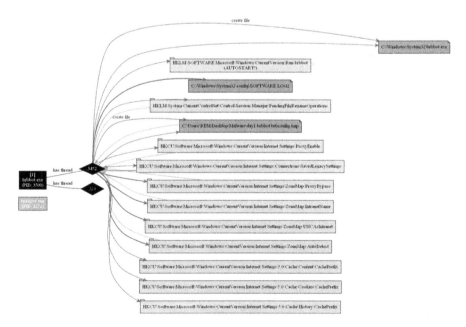

Fig. 3.9 A screenshot showing activity diagram for brbbot.exe using ProcDOT

If you pan the graph to the side, displaying its right portion that didn't fit on the screen capture above, you will see activities related to registry keys under . . , Windows\Current Version\Internet Settings. Sometimes, such events indicate attempts by malware to modify the system's Internet connectivity settings. More frequently, they are also an innocuous side effect of the program instantiating a Windows library used for interacting with websites.

ProcDOT indicated that the process tenninated itself, presumably because it received a request from the OS or another process to do that.

Wireshark

Switch to your REMnux virtual machine, and take a look at the log file that Wireshark captured when you infected the Windows VM with brbbot.exe.

The log includes an attempt to resolve the hostname brb.3dtuts.by using DNS, as captured on the screenshot below. In the case of this screenshot, the infected system has the IP address 192.168.87.135, and it treats 192.168.87.131 as its DNS server. The IP addresses in your lab are probably different (Shekhawat et al., 2019).

Note that because we haven't enabled DNS services in the lab, the response to this query is an ICMP Destination unreachable (Port unreachable) message, indicating that the system cannot process this connection attempt (Fig. 3.10).

A common practice when performing behavioral analysis is to give the specimen the network resources that it seeks, allowing it to exhibit additional characteristics. In the case of brbbot.exe, the malicious program is looking to resolve a hostname using DNS. For this to work, we need to bring a DNS server into the lab or manually modify the "hosts" file on the infected host.

You could use a full-blown DNS server in your lab. A more convenient alternative might be the fakedns utility, which automatically responds to DNS queries with the IP address of the host on which it runs. When you run fakedns on REMnux, it

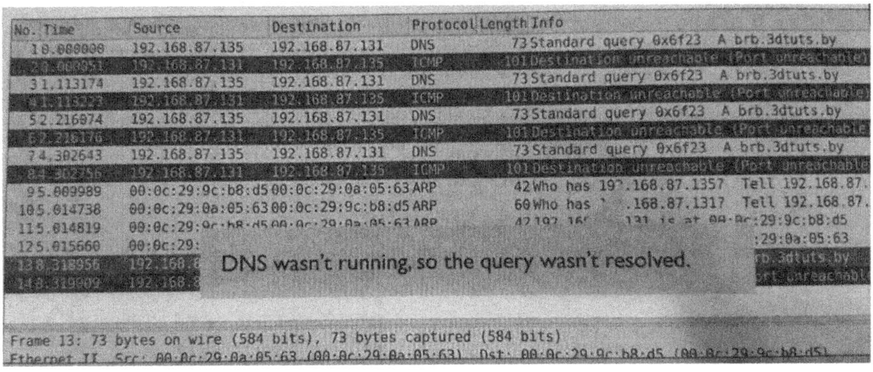

Fig. 3.10 A screenshot showing Wireshark-captured traffic and the DNS query

will listen to DNS connections on UDP port 53 and respond to all hostname-resolution queries with the IP address of your REMnux virtual machine. This way, whenever a specimen attempts to resolve a hostname, we will redirect it to your Linux VM. This approach to traffic redirection is very helpful for interacting with malware when studying its behavior in the lab.

To launch fakedns on REMnux, open a new terminal window and type fakedns. When fakedns is running, test its operation by going to your Windows REM Workstation, opening command prompt, and attempting to resolve some hostname using nslookup, for instance nslookup google.com

This query should resolve to the IP address of your REMnux virtual machine, which on this screenshot (Fig. 3.11) is 192.168.87.131. The IP address in your lab will probably be different. If nslookup fails to resolve the hostname, check TCP/IP settings within your Windows REM Workstation to confirm that its DNS server is defined as the IP address of your REMnux virtual machine.

Now that you've adjusted the configuration of your lab by bringing in a (fake) DNS server, you can repeat the experiment to see whether the specimen exhibits new behavioral characteristics.

On REMnux, start a new Wireshark capture by pressing Ctrl+E or selecting Capture > Start.

Then, switch to your Windows REM Workstation, and exit the monitoring tools you used earlier in the previous experiment with the exception of Process Hacker. In other words, quit Process Monitor and ProcDOT. Normally, you would want to save the output of these tools for later reference, but you don't need to do that in the

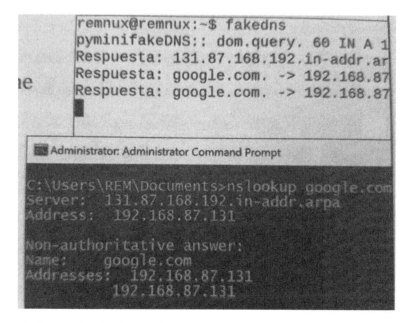

Fig. 3.11 A screenshot showing nslookup query resolving to the REMnux IP address

context of this book. It's convenient to leave Process Hacker active so that you can observe the brbbot.exe process and terminate it when you're ready to do that.

Re-infect your Windows REM Workstation virtual machine with brbbot.exe, using its shortcut as you did in the previous experiment. Normally, it would be cleaner to revert to a snapshot before re-infecting. However, in the case of this example, we know the specimen doesn't embed itself into the system in a way that would preclude us from continuing to interact with it. So, we'll save a few minutes and simply run brbbot.exe again without reverting.

After the malicious process has a chance to run for approximately half a minute, use Process Hacker to terminate it. Then, switch to your REMnux VM and stop capture in Wireshark.

Take a look at the terminal where fakedns is running to confirm that it received and responded to the request for brb.3dtuts.by. Then, spend a few moments looking through the Wireshark log. You should see successful DNS queries for brb.3dtuts.by and an attempt to establish a network connection we haven't seen earlier.

As you can see in the screenshot above (Fig. 3.12), fakedns responded to the request to resolve brb.3dtuts.by. You can see this part of the network conversation in Wireshark, too.

Your log might also include DNS queries for non-malicious hostnames, such as win10.ipv6.microsoft.com, officeclient.microsoft.com, and v10.vonex-win.data. microsoft.com. These activities are associated with normal Windows operations and constitute "noise" as far as we are concerned.

Wireshark also shows that the infected system (in this case, 192.168.87.135) tried to establish a connection to the REMnux VM (in this case, 192.168.87.131) on TCP port 80 by sending a SYN packet. Because we didn't see this connection attempt earlier, we can assume that we see it now because the specimen succeeded at resolving brb.3dtuts.by.

In other words, brbbot.exe is attempting to connect to the host it thinks is brb.3dtuts.by on TCP port 80 but is actually our REMnux virtual machine. This port is typically used for web (HTTP) traffic, though at the moment we cannot know for sure that HTTP is the protocol the specimen will use when the connection is

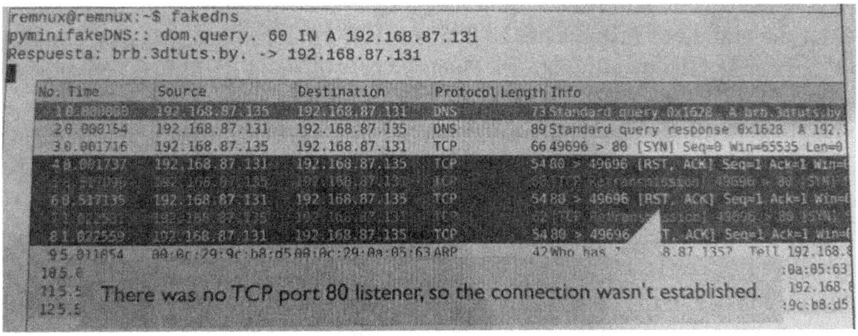

Fig. 3.12 A screenshot showing a successful DNS query using fakedns

established. Because in our lab no listener was active on TCP port 80, the REMnux VM responds with an RST, ACK packet, indicating that the connection cannot be established.

General Steps About Behavioral Analysis

Let's generalize the steps we're taking with brbbot.exe to make sure they're useful to you when you examine other samples using behavioral techniques.

The analysis process that we follow involves us gradually molding the laboratory environment as we discover new details about the malware specimen. Each step brings us closer to mimicking the runtime environment that the malicious program expects and, therefore, gently encourages the specimen to exhibit characteristics we haven't yet observed. By making one small change at a time, we can understand what aspects of the configuration influence the sample's behavior.

This methodology calls for making only one configuration change at a time so that it's easier for you to determine what specific tweak caused the new behavior you observe and helps ensure that you capture as much information as possible (Coulter et al., 2020).

This is a relatively slow but thorough process. If you're in a hurry, one way to speed up behavioral analysis is to preemptively introduce the services that you believe malware might need. In this case, you will probably see interesting behavior more quickly but might not be able to tell whether malware would have behaved differently had some of those resources been unavailable to it.

Using Process Hacker, confirm that the brbbot.exe process isn't still running on your Windows REM Workstation. If it is, terminate the process. REMnux has a web server built into it, though it's not active by default. To start the web server, go to your REMnux virtual machine, and type the command httpd start in an available terminal window. The service will run silently in the background.

Keep fakedns running in another terminal window because we want it to continue answering the DNS requests that brbbot.exe might send in the next experiment. Start a new capture in Wireshark by pressing Ctrl+E or by using Capture > Start. Switch to your Windows virtual machine, and re-infect it with brbbot.exe.

After the malicious process has a chance to run for approximately half a minute, use Process Hacker to terminate it. Then, switch to your REMnux VM and stop capture in Wireshark.

Spend a few minutes looking over the Wireshark log. This time, you may be able to see a fully established HTTP session that was, presumably, initiated by brbbot. exe to the host it thinks is brb.3dtuts.by. A convenient way to look at the payload of that connection is to right-click in Wireshark on one of the packets associated with it and select Follow TCP Stream.

As you can see in the packet capture on the screen capture above (Fig. 3.13), the infected system (192.168.87.135 in this example) succeeded at establishing a WVTP connection to the REMnux host (192.168.87.131 in this example).

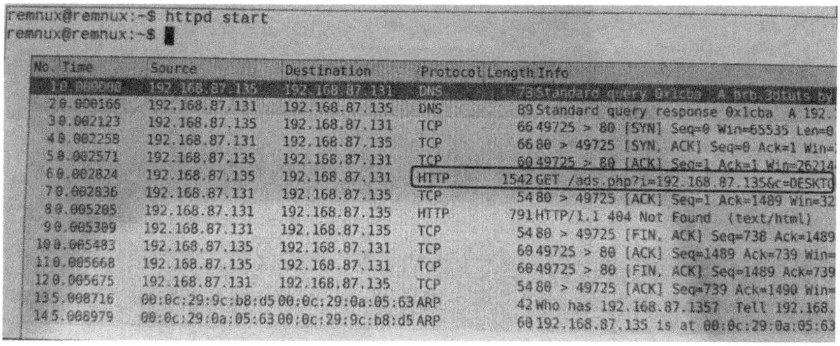

Fig. 3.13 A screenshot showing an stablished connection between the REMnux and Windows machines

The screenshot shows the partial details of the HTTP GET request that probably originates from brbbot.exe as it attempts to communicate with brb.3dtuts.by.

If you kept Wireshark capturing the network traffic for a few minutes, you would notice that the infected system sends this HTTP request approximately every 30 s.

Closer Look at HTTP Connection

For a closer look at HTTP connection, we will use Wireshark's feature Follow TCP Stream. Right-clicking a packet that's part of the HTTP connection and then selecting Follow TCP Stream present the window shown on the screen capture below. This looks like a valid HTTP request, which was probably sent by brbbot.exe to the website it believed to be brb.3dtuts.by.

The GET request is typically transmitted by the web browser to request that the web server provides the designated web page or file. In our capture, the resource that's being requested is the output of the /ads.php script (Fig. 3.14) that the bot expects to find on the web server. The bot seems to provide data to this script in the form of parameters separated by ampersands (&), which is a common way of submitting data as part of a GET request. Let's look at the data being transmitted.

The value assigned to the "i" parameter is 192.168.87.135, which is the IP address assigned to the infected Windows system in this example.

The value assigned to the "c" parameter is DESKTOP-S6JUKAN, which is the hostname of the infected Windows system in this example.

The value assigned to the "p" parameter is encoded in hexadecimal. We cannot readily tell what it is. Even if you decoded it from hex to ASCII, you wouldn't see any meaningful data. Perhaps this data is not only encoded in hex but also encrypted or obfuscated.

The /ads.php page is not present on the REMnux web server. That's why the server responded with 404 Not Found. However, we still accomplished the goal of

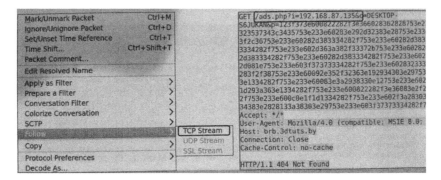

Fig. 3.14 A screenshot showing how to use the Follow-TCP-Stream feature of Wireshark

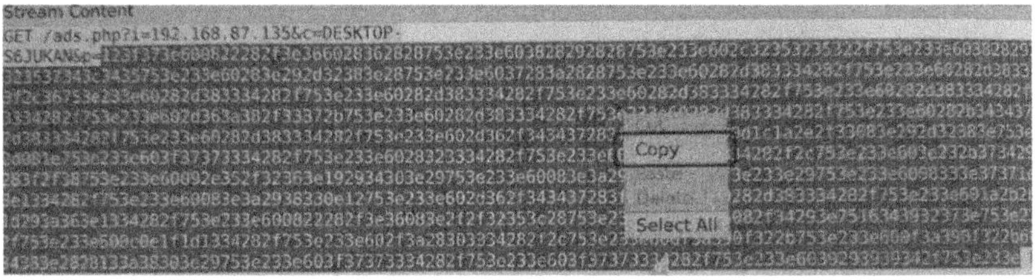

Fig. 3.15 A screenshot showing how to copy the encoded payload to the clipboard

this experiment, which was determining the purpose of the HTTP connection. Based on the data we could see, we can tell that the specimen seems to be sending information about the infected system to the attacker.

What data is brbbot sending to the attacker in the "p" parameter? We'll figure this out by looking deeper into this specimen's inner workings. So that we can decode this data later, save the hexadecimal contents of the payload.

To save the data, select the hex-encoded contents that follow the "p" parameter. (They are highlighted on the screen capture.) When highlighting, do not include the equal sign that precedes this text. Nor should you include the space at the end of the text. Right-click the highlighted text, and select Copy to copy it to the clipboard (Fig. 3.15).

After copying the encoded payload to the clipboard, switch to an open or a new terminal window without exiting Wireshark. You can now save clipboard contents to a file using a variety of methods. One approach involves using the SciTE text editor that's included in REMnux. (By the way, to make it easier to remember how to launch this tool, REMnux includes the alias Notepad that invokes SciTE.)

Use SciTE-encoded.hex to create the file into which you save the packet payload excerpt. After SciTE launches, paste clipboard contents into it and save the file. Don't forget to save! Confirm that the appropriate contents were saved in the file by looking at it with a command such as cat-encoded.hex (Fig. 3.16).

If you prefer to use command-line tools instead of SciTE, here's an alternative approach to saving the encoded contents:

coded.hex
f373e600822282f3e3660283628287532e233e603828292828753e233e602c32353235322f753e233e6038282928Z
.02c323537343c3435753e233e60283e292d32383e28753e233e6037283a2828753e233e60282d383334282f753e
3833342282f753e233e603f2c36753e233e60282d383334282f753e233e60282d383334282f753e233e60282d38L
e233e60282d383334282f753e233e60282d383334282f753e233e602d363a382f33372b753e233e60282d383334
3e60282d383334282f753e233e60282b3434437282d753e233e60282d383334282f753e233e60282d383334282f7
d362f343437283f753e233e600d1c1a2e2f33083e292d32383e753e233e600c36320b292d081e753e233e603f37
753e233e60283233334282f753e233e602f3a28303334282f2c753e233e603e232b3734293e29753e233e603628J
33e60092e352f32363e192934303e29753e233e60083e3a29383312353f3e233e29753e233e6008333e37371e23

Fig. 3.16 A screenshot showing the encoded payload of brbbot.exe

1. Create a new file by typing cat > encoded.hex and pressing Enter.
2. Paste clipboard contents into the terminal window (Edit > Paste).
3. Press CtTI+D to indicate that this is the end of the data you'll be placing inside the encoded hex file.

You can attempt to convert contents of the encoded.hex file into ASCII. A quick way to do this is to use the xxd -r -p encoded.hex command. However, in the case of processing the encoded.hex file, this command produces gibberish output. This result indicates that the data transmitted by brbbot.exe in the "p" parameter isn't simple ASCI text encoded as hex (Wang et al., 2019).

Summary of Findings About brbbot.exe Through Behavioral Analysis

The specimen generates an encoded brbconfig.tmp file when infecting a system. It reads the file after creating it. The malicious program also creates a key named "brbbot" under the ... \Run registry key to maintain a persistent presence on the system. The specimen attempts to connect to brb.3dtuts.by using HTTP after successfully resolving this hostname using DNS.

When making the I-WRP connection, the specimen sends a GET request for "/ads.php" from the web server, specifying several parameters as part of the request. Two of the parameters that we could see correspond to data points about the infected system, which is apparently transmitted ("texfiltrated") to the adversary. The third parameter is encoded, but even when decoded from hex, it still appears obfuscated or encrypted. We saved the contents of this parameter in the encoded.hex file for future analysis.

These observations help us understand the nature of brbbot.exe and the threat that it might pose to our enterprise. They also expand upon the earlier theories regarding IOCs, which we formed during static properties analysis. Now, we know that looking for specific files, process names, and network connection properties has a reasonable chance of enabling us to detect this specimen or its use in our environment.

Perhaps more importantly, by walking through these behavioral analysis steps with respect to brbbot.exe, we learned key principles that will assist you in future situations when you examine other malware samples.

Summary

Behavioral malware analysis is an excellent technique to aid in learning about the nature of a malware specimen and its network communication patterns. Behavioral analysis can be useful to expand upon and validate theories regarding IOCs, which were found during static analysis phase. Thus, combining the findings from both static analysis and behavioral analysis will help gain more insight and understanding of the inner working of a malware file. It's also noteworthy that behavioral analysis has its limitations because most modern malware encrypts, obfuscates, or otherwise encodes its data when communicating over the network with malware infrastructure (command and control server or C2 servers). Therefore, to understand how a malware binary encrypts network traffic and what data is encrypted, we will need to know how to perform code analysis (reverse-code engineering). In the next chapter, we will learn the concepts, tools, and techniques to perform code analysis.

References

Afianian, A., Niksefat, S., Sadeghiyan, B., & Baptiste, D. (2020). Malware dynamic analysis evasion techniques: A survey. *ACM Computing Surveys, 52*(6), 1–28. https://doi.org/10.1145/3365001

Coulter, R., Han, Q.-L., Pan, L., Zhang, J., & Xiang, Y. (2020). Code analysis for intelligent cyber systems: A data-driven approach. *Information Sciences, 524*, 46–58. https://doi.org/10.1016/j.ins.2020.03.036

Shekhawat, A. S., Troia, F. D., & Stamp, M. (2019). Feature analysis of encrypted malicious traffic. *Expert Systems with Applications, 125*, 130–141. https://doi.org/10.1016/j.eswa.2019.01.064

Ul Haq, I., Chica, S., Caballero, J., & Jha, S. (2018). Malware lineage in the wild. *Computers & Security, 78*, 347–363. https://doi.org/10.1016/j.cose.2018.07.012

Wang, L., Wang, B., Zhang, J., Liu, J., & Miao, Q. (2019). Cuckoo-based malware dynamic analysis. *International Journal of Performability Engineering, 15*(3), 772–781. https://doi.org/10.23940/ijpe.19.03.p6.772781

Zhang, X., & Song, X. (2020). Stability analysis of a dynamical model for malware propagation with generic nonlinear countermeasure and infection probabilities. *Security and Communication Networks, 2020*, 1–7. https://doi.org/10.1155/2020/8859883

Chapter 4
Principles of Code-Level Analysis

Principles of Code-Level Analysis

Static properties analysis and behavioral analysis are excellent techniques to understand the basic characteristics and functionality of malware; however, these techniques alone do not offer all the needed information to fully understand the malware's functionality. Malware authors often write their malicious code in a high-level language, such as C or C++, which is compiled to an executable program using a compiler (Monnappa, 2018). Security analysts do not have access to the source code during the malware analysis process; they only have access to the malicious executable. To better understand the critical dimensions of a malicious specimen as well as its inner workings, we will need to take our analysis efforts to the next level: code analysis.

We've learned quite a bit about brbbot.exe through behavioral analysis and, in the process, experimented with several useful tools and techniques. Yet, we still have some answered questions regarding this specimen. It's time to look at its code to see what mysteries it might reveal.

Because we couldn't evoke any more activity from the specimen using behavioral techniques, we know this is a good time to start the code analysis phase. Code analysis enables us to answer questions about the characteristics of brbbot.exe. Our pursuit of answers to these questions will give us the opportunity to learn about the essential aspects of code analysis tools and techniques.

When dealing with a compiled executable that might be malicious, you're unlikely to be in a situation in which you have the source code to the specimen. Therefore, you'll need to rely on tools that help you understand the low-level assembly instructions that comprise the executable. To accomplish this, analysts often start examining the program's code by focusing on instructions or code blocks that represent a pattern or behavior that catches their attention.

© The Author(s), under exclusive license to Springer Nature Switzerland AG 2022   37
M. Omar, *Defending Cyber Systems through Reverse Engineering of Criminal Malware*, SpringerBriefs in Computer Science,
https://doi.org/10.1007/978-3-031-11626-1_4

Disassemblers and debuggers are helpful for such tasks. We'll use some of the better-known tools in this category: IDA—the freeware version (https://www.hex-rays.com/products/ida) and x64dbg (http://x64dbg.com).

You might want to include other tools of this nature in your toolkit; however, we won't have the opportunity to discuss them in the book. They include:

- WinDbg: A powerful and free Windows debugger from Microsoft (https://developer.microsoft.com/en-us/windows/hardware/windows-driver-kit).
- Radare2: An open-source toolkit for Windows and Linux, installed on REMnux (http://rada.re).
- Binary Ninja: A commercial disassembler that's especially strong for automated analysis tasks (https://binary.ninja).
- Hopper: A commercial disassembler and decompiler that runs on OSX and Linux (https://www.hopperapp.com).

People who feel comfortable reading assembly code might prefer to start examining a malicious program by loading it into a disassembler or debugger. However, the majority of malware analysts will find it easier to start with static properties and behavioral analysis, which reveal some aspects of the specimen's functionality and help determine what code to examine for further details.

When analysts use the term disassembling, they are referring to the process of translating binary machine-level instructions that the processor understands to assembly language code that's easier for humans to understand. Tools that accomplish such translation are called disassemblers. A modem disassembler is expected to not only perform the core translation work but also to intelligently distinguish between code and data embedded into the executable, provide comments and labels, and otherwise help the analyst's reverse-engineering efforts (Coulter et al., 2020).

In this context, static analysis involves using a disassembler to examine the specimen's code without actually executing it. In contrast, dynamic analysis involves actually running the program while examining its activities at the assembly level. Debuggers are tools that are designed to perform such tasks; they have built-in disassemblers and can accommodate static and dynamic reverse-engineering activities. x64dbg is one such tool, which we're about to start using.

X64dbg Explained

x64dbg is a capable debugger for Windows executables. It's an open-source project that is being rapidly developed. It provides a convenient user interface that reverse-engineers can use to navigate through the specimen to perform static and, perhaps even more importantly, dynamic code-level analysis. x64dbg enables its users to install plugins and write scripts that extend the debugger's built-in capabilities (Yakura et al., 2019).

x64dbg can handle 32-bit and 64-bit code. To accomplish this, it's actually shipped with two separate programs: x32dbg for 32-bit executables and x64dbg for

64-bit executables. However, the name x64dbg is still used when referring to the overall tool. x64dbg is available free from http://x64dbg.com.

We'll start getting to know this handy tool in the context of brbbot.exe. We will load this specimen into x64dbg on the Windows REM Workstation. One way to do this is to drag the icon of the brbbot.exe file (or the icon of the shortcut to this file) and drop it on top of the x64dbg icon. Another is to open the x64dbg application by itself and load the desired file using File > Open (F3). When loading an executable, x64dbg typically pauses in the beginning of the program's code before it has a chance to run. This gives us the opportunity to decide where and how to begin examining the specimen.

The disassembler built into x64dbg is visible on the CPU tab (x64dbg calls these tabs "views"). Like most other disassemblers, it shows one assembly instruction per line. The second column in the disassembler shows hexadecimal values that represent the relative addresses, sometimes called offsets, of the instructions; the third column shows space-separated groupings of hexadecimal values that represent the instructions themselves, which the processor can recognize and execute. The next column shows the version of those instructions in human-readable assembly language. The rightmost columns show comments, many of which x64dbg automatically inserts to aid your efforts (Sibi Chakkaravarthy et al., 2019).

Because assembly is a low-level language, expect to encounter difficulties understanding the meaning of some of the more cryptic portions of the code when looking at them statically. This is where the dynamic capabilities of a debugger such as x64dbg can help.

Debuggers enable you to execute malware under highly controlled conditions, with the ability to step through the program as slowly as one instruction at a time. You probably won't have the patience to manually step through every single instruction, so you can take advantage of the debugger's capability to set breakpoints that interrupt the execution of the program at specific workflow branches. When stepping through portions of the program, you can peek at its memory and register contents and even modify this information on the fly (Imran et al., 2017).

You can see the many ways in which x64dbg enables you to interact with the debugged specimen if you glance at the Debug menu of the tool. You can choose to run the malicious process, or you can single-step through its instructions one at a time. You can direct the debugger to pause the execution of the debugged process by setting a breakpoint that defines the circumstances under which x64dbg will pause the specimen and give you control. If single-stepping, you can decide whether you wish to drill into functions to see what happens within them or whether you wish to execute them in one step (Fig. 4.1).

These capabilities give you visibility into how the specimen interacts with its environment as it runs and how it manipulates data. A debugger enables you to modify many aspects of the process, tweaking its code and data according to your objectives. The file menu captured in the screenshot above offers only a brief peek into x64dbg's capabilities. There is much to learn about this powerful debugger (Fig. 4.2).

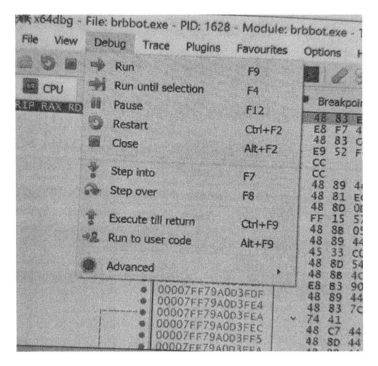

Fig. 4.1 A screenshot of the interface of x64dbg and on how to run code from there

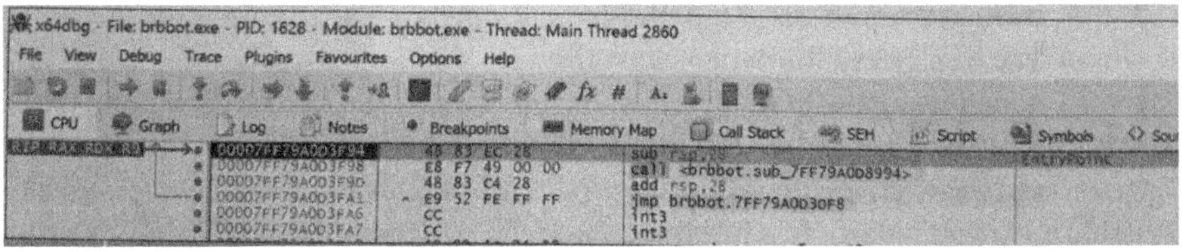

Fig. 4.2 A screenshot showing brbbot.exe loaded into x64dbg

Deep-Dive into x64dbg

We'll start becoming familiar with x64dbg by pursuing a specific objective: Decode contents of the brbconfig.tmp file. Recall that in the ProcDOT graph, we saw that brbbot.exe created this file and then read from it. It's likely that the specimen is using this file to store some configuration details. However, we don't know how the file's contents are encoded.

This is the point at which a debugger can help. We can use x64dbg to set a breakpoint on the code that brbbot.exe might use to read brbconfig.tmp from the file system. That should bring us to the general vicinity of the code the specimen uses to decipher the file's contents. At that point, we can use the debugger to "spy" on the specimen as it decodes the file, so we can determine its contents (Alaeiyan et al., 2019).

How might we be able to locate where brbbot.exe reloads brbconfig.tmp? One approach is to look for references to Windows APIs that the specimen could use to perform this action. As we covered in the "Static Properties Analysis" section, you can see such APIs by looking at the specimen's import table using tools such as PeStudio.

We will load brbbot.exe from the %AppData% folder into PeStudio on Windows REM Workstation. Go to the imports area, and scroll through the listed symbol names to locate those that might be used to read the file. One API that stands out, as captured on the screen capture, is ReadFile.

According to Microsoft, the ReadFile function is implemented in the kernel32. dll library in Windows. Its purpose is to read "data from the specified file or input/ output (I/O) device" (https://msdn.microsoft.com/en-us/library/windows/desktop/ aa365467(v=vs.85).aspx).

If our goal is to locate brbbot.exe code that loads brbconfig.tmp, we can attempt to achieve it by using x64dbg to set a breakpoint on API calls that can accomplish such actions. Specifically, we'll set a breakpoint on ReadFile. This way, once the specimen calls ReadFile to read a file, x64dbg will pause the execution of brbbot. exe and enable us to see what file is being read and how its contents are being processed.

To accomplish this, we will exit PeStudio and switch to the x64dbg window, which should still have brbbot.exe loaded in it. How should we set the breakpoint?

Most of the features of x64dbg are accessible using its graphical user interface (GUI). However, given the many tabs, windows, toolbars, and menus that comprise the GUI, it's often faster and more convenient to interact with the debugger by typing commands into the Command window located in the bottom-left corner of the x64dbg window.

For instance, you can set a breakpoint at the beginning of the ReadFile function by typing the following command in the Command window, as shown on the screenshot below:

We will press enter after typing this command in the Command window (Fig. 4.3).

Conveniently, the debugger automatically locates this function name in the appropriate Windows library, without requiring that you specify the DLL name. It's important to note that in the API call names, the case of the letters matters. So, we have to make sure we type uppercase R and F when entering ReadFile. The case of the letters that comprise the command itself (e.g., SetBPX) is not important. By the way, x64dbg sometimes offers several ways to specify the same command. Alternative ways of running SetBPX are commands bpx and bp.

To list the currently defined breakpoints, we will navigate to the Breakpoints tab of x64dbg's window. We see the kernel32.dll.ReadFile entry there, as shown at the bottom of the screenshot above.

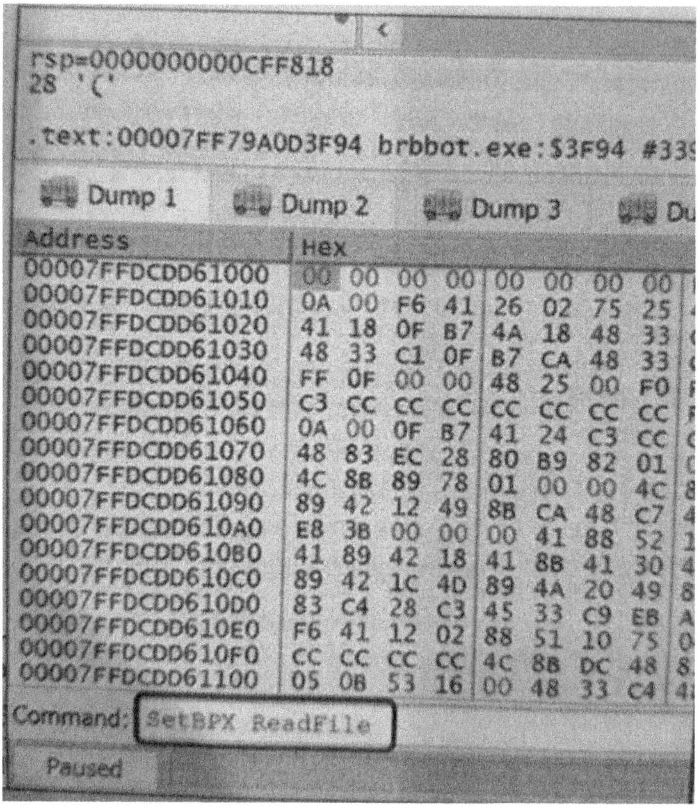

Fig. 4.3 A screenshot showing how to set a breakpoint at the beginning of the ReadFile function

Now that we have set the breakpoint on ReadFile, we will run the specimen within x64dbg. We can accomplish this by using the Debug > Run menu, pressing F9, or typing the run command in the debugger's Command window.

The specimen should start executing and then pause after its code makes the ReadFile call. You should find yourself in x64dbg's CPU tab, with the program paused at the following instruction:

imp qword per dB: [<&Rea

If you glance at the title of the x64dbg window, you'll notice that the code the debugger is displaying is inside kernel32.dll. Our specimen loaded this library when its process was created, and it's now invoking the ReadFile function that's implemented within that DLL.

Note the RIP pointer on the left side of the CPU window (Fig. 4.4). This arrow designates the current instruction. In this context, current means the instruction that will be executed next by the debugged program. RIP is the name of the register on a 64-bit platform that contains the address of the current instruction. On a 32-bit platform, the register that has this responsibility is EIP.

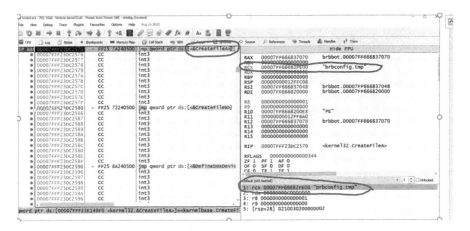

Fig. 4.4 A screenshot showing the "create file" function and how it's used to create the "brbbot-config.tmp" file

Registers, by the way, are special locations in the CPU that are very efficient at storing small amounts as data.

According to Microsoft's documentation on ReadFile, this function expects to receive several parameters, as captured in the screenshot (Fig. 4.5). The first parameter should be a handle that points to the resource from which ReadFile needs to read the contents. The parameter is called hFile (https://msdn.microsoft.com/en-us/library/windows/desktop/aa365467.aspx).

Assembly code can pass parameters to a function in several ways; note that 64-bit code often uses the register rcx for supplying the first parameter to a function (An Investigation of Cryptojacking, 2019).

An easy way to see in x64dbg which parameters are being passed to the function is to glance at the middle region on the right side of the CPU tab, captured on the top-right portion of the screenshot. Notice that the rcx register contains the value 110 in our example. This value acts as the numeric identifier of the handle that's being supplied to ReadFile as the hFile parameter.

The next screen capture (Fig. 4.6) will explain how to determine where this handle is pointing.

One way to determine where handle 110 is pointing is to go to the Handles tab in x64dbg, right-click there, and select Refresh. x64dbg will provide information about active handles for the process you're currently debugging. Look for handle 110 in the resulting listing. As you can see at the bottom of the screen capture, that handle points to the brbconfig.tmp file, as we were hoping it would.

An alternative approach to looking at handle details is to examine the malicious process using Process Hacker. To do that, minimize x64dbg, go to Process Hacker, locate the brbbot.exe process, right-click on it, and select Properties. Then go to the Handles tab. As you can see here, the tool confirms that this handle is pointing to brbconfig.tmp.

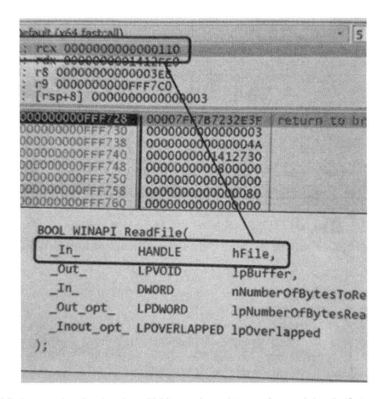

Fig. 4.5 A screenshot showing that x64-bit uses the register rcx for supplying the first parameter to a function

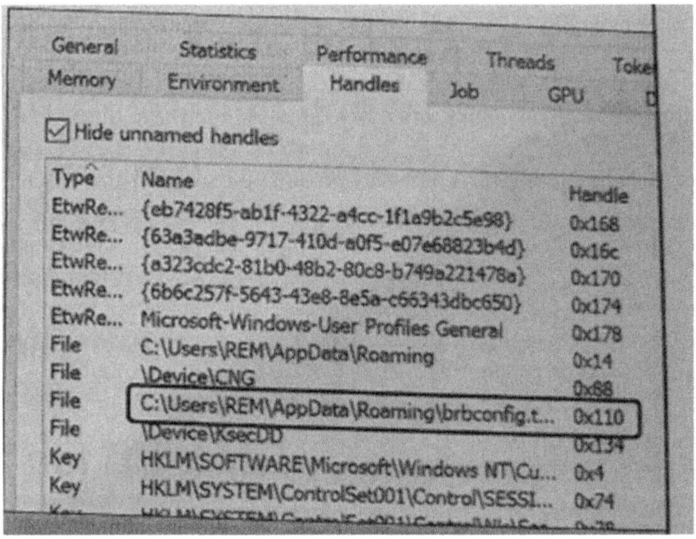

Fig. 4.6 A screenshot showing where this handle is pointing

Dissecting brbbot.exe

Now, we know we're on the right track. In other words, we're in the vicinity of the code that is responsible for reading and hopefully decoding this file's contents.

Our specimen is presently paused in the beginning of executing ReadFile within kerneB2.d11. Our objective is to examine the code implemented by the developer (called user code) of brbbot.exe to see what the specimen does with the contents after they've been read. To accomplish this, we want to allow ReadFile to finish executing and pause once the program reaches user code. One way to do that is to go to the Debug menu of x64dbg and select Run to user code (Alt+F9).

If you'd like to better understand how the specimen found itself in the beginning of ReadFile, take a look at the Call Stack tab before allowing the code to continue running; this view shows the path of nested functions in reverse chronological order that the program executed before pausing at the current place in the program. Envision the malicious code calling one function, that function calling another, that one calling another, and that function calling ReadFile. Here is an example of how to interpret the contents of this tab.

The top line of the Call Stack in our example shows that ReadFile will return to the instruction at 7FF79AOD2E3F inside the body of brbbot.exe. The address 7FFDCD604750 on that line indicates that this is where we're presently paused; it matches the beginning of ReadFile.

The next line of the Call Stack shows that the function will return to 7FF79AOD1323 when it finishes executing. That function will return to 7FF79AOD2823 and so on. This information can help you navigate through the specimen's code if you wanted to determine how you ended up in the current part of the program. Switch to the CPU tab, and select Debug > Run to user code (Alt+F9). This will allow ReadFile to finish executing.

This step should bring you to the instruction immediately after ReadFile was invoked within brbbot.exe.

Per the instructions on the above screen capture, x64dbg should pause after returning from ReadFile, which is the instruction test eax.

If you scroll up just one line in the disassembler area of the CPU tab, you will see the instruction that invoked the ReadFile function from which we just "climbed out." That instruction was

call qword per dg:

The call operand in this instruction is the typical way in which functions are invoked in assembly.

Our observations so far suggest that we're in the area of brbbot.exe where the specimen is reading the brbconfig.tmp file. Now, look a bit further in the code listing within x64dbg's disassembler. Roughly 15 instructions further, there is a call to an interesting function named CryptDecrypt:

call qword per dB:

According to Microsoft, this API call "decrypts data previously encrypted by using the CryptEncrypt function," which is also a part of the Windows cryptographic API set (https://msdn.microsoft.com/enus/library/windows/desktop/aa379913.aspx).

Based on this information, we can conclude that brbbot.exe uses CryptDecrypt to decrypt contents of the brbconfig.tmp, which it just read by calling ReadFile.

We can use x64dbg to look at the results of CryptDecrypt, in the hope that they will reveal decoded brbconfig.tmp contents. To do this, click on the test eax, eax instruction that immediately follows the call to CryptDecrypt to highlight its line. Then, go to the Debug menu, and select Run until selection or press F4.

This selection will direct x64dbg to execute brbbot.exe code until it reaches that instruction, at which point the debugger will pause. This pause should occur immediately after the call to CryptDecrypt.

As you can see on the screen capture above (Fig. 4.7), the specimen paused after executing CryptDecrypt. Now, we can examine brbbot.exe's runtime environment to determine the results of the CryptDecrypt function. Microsoft's documentation for CryptDecrypt indicates that it places decrypted contents into the buffer whose address was passed to this function as the fifth parameter named pbData. In our sample, this parameter ends up pointing to the top of the stack, which is where you will see a pointer to the decrypted string after the CryptDecrypt call. As captured on the screen capture, the memory address stored in that parameter appears to contain a readable string, which we will examine now.

The bottom of the screen capture displays the full string that brbbot.exe decoded after reading its encrypted version from the brbconfig.tmp file.

This observation confirms that brbconfig.tmp contains configuration details for the specimen. The file's contents specify what page on the adversary's web server it should access, what commands the attacker can supply to it (presumably via that

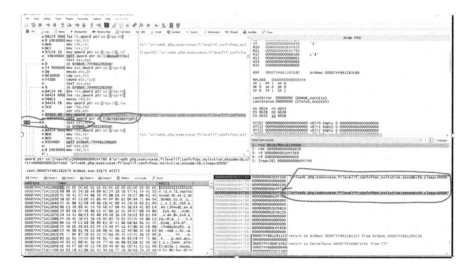

Fig. 4.7 A screenshot showing the result of the CryptDecrypt function after the breakpoint

web page), and how often the specimen should retrieve the web page. The configuration also includes the value "encode," which seems to include some sort of an encoding key (5b). It makes sense that the attacker would want to protect this sensitive data by encrypting the contents of the brbconfig.tmp file.

When we combine this analysis with our behavioral observations, we can conclude that the specimen contains this file's contents embedded into its executable file. When it runs, brbbot.exe saves these configuration details to the file system and then reads them from the file system. It is possible that if a version of this file is already present, the specimen will use that file's configuration instead of the defaults embedded into its executable file (Afianian et al., 2020).

We'll further discuss the contents of brbconfig.tmp a bit later in this section.

We just learned how to use a debugger, such as x64dbg, to observe the specimen's interactions with its runtime environment. This tool enabled us to "spy" on the parameters the program passes to external functions, as well as to examine the return values of API calls.

API Monitor

We can employ another approach to accomplish this goal if it is sufficient for us to pay attention to the functions that the specimen calls from external DLLs without having visibility into the program's interactions with internally defined functions. One free but powerful tool we can use for examining such API calls made by the processes running on our Windows laboratory system is API Monitor. This tool is available free from http://www.rohitab.com/apimonitor.

To become familiar with API Monitor, we can use (the x64 version of) this tool to decode brbconfig.tmp contents by observing how brbbot.exe calls CryptDecrypt. The general approach is not very different from how we performed this task using x64dbg. However, accomplishing this task with API Monitor usually involves fewer steps and, therefore, tends to be simpler and faster. (If trying these steps in your lab, be sure to terminate brbbot.exe, perhaps by exiting x64dbg, before continuing.)

Prior to monitoring a process in API Monitor, we need to select the API calls we would like to observe. The easiest way to do this involves taking advantage of the API categories that the tool displays in its API Filter window, which is captured on the left side of the screenshot above. In our example, if we would like to observe how brbbot.exe decrypts content using API capabilities of Windows, we don't even need to know about the CryptDecrypt function. Instead, we can navigate in the API Filter window to Security and Identity, and select the Cryptography category.

Next, we select Monitor New Process from the File menu or from the link in the middle of the API Monitor window. Then point API Monitor to %AppData%\brbbot.exe in the Process area, and click OK. The tool also enables you to "spy" on the currently running processes by attaching to them. However, launching the process from within API Monitor makes it less likely that you will miss the relevant API call.

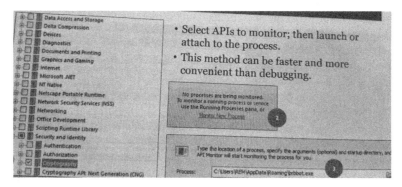

Fig. 4.8 A screenshot showing the crypto API calls made by brbbot.exe

Whenever the brbbot.exe process makes an API call that falls into the Cryptography category, API Monitor lists that call in the Summary window shown on top of the screen capture above (Fig. 4.8). In our example, the tool observed several such API calls, including CryptDecrypt.

For each of these calls, API Monitor displays what parameters were passed to the external function and what data was retuned by the function.

Clicking CryptDecrypt in the Summary window directs API Monitor to display contents of the buffer that the call operated upon. As you can see on the above screen capture, the buffer contains decrypted contents of the brbconfig.tmp file, which is consistent with what we uncovered with the help of x64dbg earlier.

As you can see, API Monitor can be fast and convenient when you wish to monitor the specimen's use of standard Windows APIs. However, sometimes you need the visibility and control that you can only get with a debugger such as x64dbg. Recall that, in an earlier experiment, we used Wireshark to capture the data that brbbot.exe was sending from the infected system. A portion of that data was hex-encoded, but decoding it into ASCII didn't produce a meaningful result. We saved these contents into the encoded.hex file.

Now that we've decrypted the contents of brbconfig.tmp, we see a reference to an "encode" value of 5b. This value could be the key for decoding the data exfiltrated by the specimen. But if it's the key, which algorithm might be using it? Malware authors can use numerous algorithms for concealing data. Some of these approaches can be relatively complex, as was the case with the CryptEncrypt/CryptDecrypt method used to protect brbconfig.tmp. Others can be relatively simple. One approach that's often used by malware authors to obfuscate strings—mostly due to the simplicity of its implementation—uses the Boolean XOR operator to change each character in the original string by XORing it with a 1-byte key value. To decode the XOR-encoded string, the malicious program performs the same operation, XORing each character within the obfuscated string with the value of the key. The key is chosen by the malware author and might be embedded within the malicious executable or stored in a configuration file (Afianian et al., 2020). Another simple obfuscation approach rotates each byte in the string by some number of bits to the right or to the left. This algorithm is called ROR (rotate right) or ROL (rotate left), depending on the direction in which the rotation occurs. Another common approach called ROT rotates alphabet characters (A–Z and a–z) by a certain number of positions within the alphabet.

We can try applying the simple XOR 1-byte key to the encoded.hex file we created earlier to see whether it works.

Finding the right approach to decoding data often involves some trial and error, which in turn frequently depends on making educated guesses. In the case of brbbot. exe, we've discovered a 1-byte key value. We also know that malware authors frequently use a simple XOR-based algorithm to conceal strings. That might be a good approach to try to see whether it works in our example.

A simple way to accomplish this is to use the command xxd -r -p on REMnux, as shown on the screen capture below (Fig. 4.9) to create the encoded.raw file.

The tool xxd can be used for dumping binary files into readable hex. In this example, we're using the -r parameter to do the reverse—convert a text file that contains hex values into a binary file. (See https://www.linuxjournal.com/content/ doing-reverse-hex-dump for more information on this technique.)

To decode the raw data using XOR, we use a tool called translate.py. It's installed on REMnux and is also available as a free download from https://blog.didierstevens. com/programs/translate. According to this tool's web page, it is designed "to perform bitwise operations on files (like XOR, ROL/ROR, You specify the bitwise operation to perform as a Python expression, and pass it as a command-line argument."

The expression to decode the data stored in encoded.raw using the common XOR-based algorithm and the key 0x5b is byte 0x5b. The caret character ($^\wedge$) indicates the XOR operand. This slide shows how to use translate.py to decode the data and store the result in the decoded.txt file.

An alternative to using xxd and translate.py is to use the following regular expression:

perl -pes/ .) /chr (hex ($1) $^\wedge$ Ox5b) /ge encoded. hex > decoded. Txt

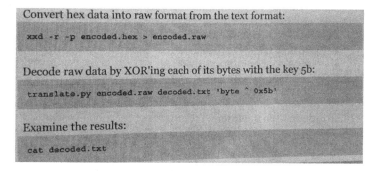

Fig. 4.9 A screenshot showing how to create the encoded file using xxd tool

```
remnux@remnux:~$ xxd -r -p encoded.hex > encoded.raw
remnux@remnux:~$ translate.py encoded.raw decoded.txt 'byte ^ 0x5b'
remnux@remnux:~$ cat decoded.txt
dle;System;smss.exe;csrss.exe;wininit.exe;csrss.exe;winlogon.exe;services.exe;lsass.exe;
vchost.exe;svchost.exe;dwm.exe;svchost.exe;svchost.exe;svchost.exe;svchost.exe;svchost.e
e;vmacthlp.exe;svchost.exe;svchost.exe;spoolsv.exe;svchost.exe;svchost.exe;vmtoolsd.exe;
GAuthService.exe;WmiPrvSE.exe;dllhost.exe;sihost.exe;taskhostw.exe;explorer.exe;msdtc.ex
;RuntimeBroker.exe;SearchIndexer.exe;ShellExperienceHost.exe;SearchUI.exe;vmtoolsd.exe;s
chost.exe;ApplicationFrameHost.exe;SystemSettings.exe;WinStore.Mobile.exe;dllhost.exe;ta
khostw.exe;WUDFHost.exe;TabTip.exe;TabTip32.exe;TrustedInstaller.exe;TiWorker.exe;Proces
Hacker.exe;Procmon.exe;Procmon64.exe;WmiPrvSE.exe;Regshot-x64-ANSI.exe;dllhost.exe;dllho
```

Fig. 4.10 A screenshot showing the contents of the decoded file using the python script translate.py

As you can see on the screenshot above (Fig. 4.10), the decoded data represents a listing of executables. These match the listing of the processes that run on the host infected by brbbot.exe. The adversary could benefit from having this information because it provides useful details regarding the business purpose of the system, the defenses that might need to be thwarted in follow-up attacks, and the opportunities for additional exploitation of the victim's system. We learned a fair bit about our specimen by performing code-level analysis steps described in this section. We were able to decrypt the contents of the brbconfig.tmp file that we observed during behavioral analysis, we confirmed that brbbot.exe uses this file for its default configuration, and we spotted within that file information that helped us deobfuscate the data that the specimen attempted to exfiltrate to the adversary. We even saw keywords in the configuration file that suggested that the specimen could receive commands from the adversary, in which case brbbot.exe might be acting as a backdoor.

Perhaps even more importantly, when pursuing these bits of information about brbbot.exe, we became familiar with some of the more fundamental aspects of code analysis, leaning heavily toward dynamic code analysis we can perform with the help of a debugger. We learned how to use some capabilities of x64dbg to observe how the specimen interacts with its runtime environment using Windows API calls, how to slow down the execution of the program with the help of breakpoints, and how to use these capabilities to decode concealed file contents.

Interactive Behavioral Analysis

This section will give us the opportunity to spend more time interacting with brbbot. exe, with the focus of better understanding C2 mechanisms of malicious programs. We will also discuss additional approaches to intercepting network traffic in our lab to facilitate such interactivity.

In the earlier sections, we already saw how we can perform behavioral analysis by mimicking inside our lab the Internet resource the specimen wishes to access. By redirecting the malicious network connection to a server and service that we control, we give the specimen the opportunity to exchange data with the server, which enables us to better understand its capabilities and to evoke additional behavioral characteristics. This way, we can learn about the program's network-centric activities, such as command and control, data exfiltration, and attempts to download other software.

Our decisions about the network connections we wanted to intercept were based on earlier analysis that might have been based on static properties, behavioral, and even code analysis. Successful redirection of these connections enables us to validate whether our earlier theories regarding the specimen's functionality were correct.

For example, we will begin this section by interacting with brbbot.exe to determine whether we're right about the C2 commands it might be able to receive from the adversary. Afterward, we will look at additional examples and techniques that involve redirecting malicious network connections in our lab so that we can better understand the nature of the specimen.

When we decrypted the brbconfig.tmp file, we noticed the use of keywords that were indicative of the commands an attacker might want to send to a backdoor, such as "exec" (execute a program), "file" (might be an instruction to download or upload file), "confr" (perhaps a way to update the bot's configuration details), and "exit" (tell the brbbot.exe process to exit).

It seems that the brbconfig.tmp file enables the attacker to define which keywords correspond to these commands. For instance, the keyword "cexe" corresponds to the command "exec," the keyword "elif'" corresponds to the command "file," and so on. Attackers typically provide such commands over the network and find it convenient to change the keywords used to invoke the commands if they want to evade intrusion detection or anti-virus detection.

Modern command and control functionality often entail remotely interacting with infected systems using HTTP (or HTTPS). To accomplish this, the malicious program periodically polls the adversary's web server using HTTP requests, downloading a page that includes commands as shown on the screen capture below (Fig. 4.11).

Now, let's consider how the adversary might issue commands to brbbot.exe. We haven't seen any network communications associated with the specimen beyond the DNS query for brb.3dtuts.by and the HTTP GET request shown on the above slide. Therefore, it is likely that the attacker provides the specimen with commands in the response to this GET request.

We can use the web server built into REMnux to experiment with command handling of brbbot.exe by embedding potential C2 commands into the /ads.php file and allowing the specimen to download it.

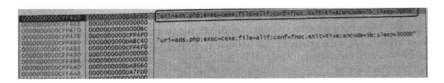

Fig. 4.11 A screenshot showing how the malware contacts the adversary's web server to execute commands

Let's create a file on REMnux upon which brbbot.exe might act and then allow the specimen to download it.

Also, fakedns should already be running from our earlier experiments.

On our Windows REM Workstation, we will launch Process Hacker if it isn't already running. Then, re-infect the virtual machine with brbbot.exe. We should observe an instance of Notepad launching on the infected VM. Note that the specimen seems to download ads.php every 30 seconds. You could confirm this by sniffing the network using Wireshark. Therefore, it will spawn a new notepad.exe process every half a minute. We can observe these activities using Process Hacker.

As another experiment, we can check how brbbot.exe handles the exit command that, according to brbconfig.tmp, is represented by the tixe keyword.

Before doing that, we will remove the ads.php file. Then, create a new version of that file to contain the tixe keyword, as shown on the screen capture below (Fig. 4.12).

When brbbot.exe receives this command in response to its HTTP GET request, the specimen's process exits. You can observe this using Process Hacker, as illustrated on the right side of this screen capture below (Fig. 4.13).

After we've confirmed that brbbot.exe received the exit command, we will turn off the web server on REMnux by issuing the httpd stop command in the REMnux terminal window. This way, if you experiment with brbbot.exe later, it will have a chance to run instead of immediately exiting when it downloads the tixe command through the ads.php file.

After completing the recent steps in exploring brbbot.exe's C2 capabilities, we have a reasonably solid understanding of the specimen's capabilities, which inform our understanding of the context within which this malicious software is likely used. These findings are based on the combination of behavioral and code analysis steps that we've been performing throughout this section.

brbbot.exe C2 Capabilities

We've just confirmed that brbbot.exe receives commands from the adversary by downloading a file through an outbound HTTP request. The commands enable the attacker to take several actions on the infected system, including executing arbitrary programs on the infected system. These capabilities allow the adversary to use brbbot.exe as a backdoor for controlling an individual host. Moreover, this C2 mechanism could be used for controlling a large number of infected hosts (let's call them a botnet) because each of them will be able to connect to the malicious web server, download the ads.php file, and act according to its contents.

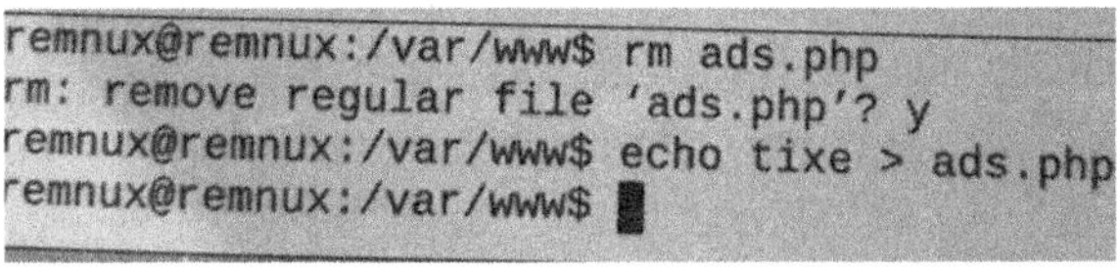

Fig. 4.12 A screenshot showing how to remove the ads.php file

```
remnux@remnux:/var/www$ rm ads.php
rm: remove regular file 'ads.php'? y
remnux@remnux:/var/www$ echo tixe > ads.php
remnux@remnux:/var/www$
```

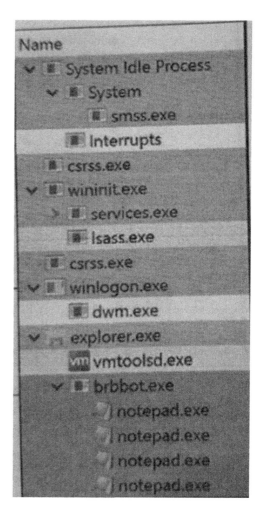

Fig. 4.13 A screenshot showing brbbot.exe exits using Process Hacker

Earlier analysis also indicated that the adversary can change the keywords that represent C2 commands through the brbconfig.tmp file. This means that if we created IOCs (or network intrusion detection signatures) that look for keywords such as cexe or tixe, we might fail to locate brbbot.exe's activities if the adversary supplies the specimen with a different configuration file.

Overall, the capabilities of brbbot.exe make it a useful tool for performing malicious actions relatively early in the infection chain. The type of data it exfiltrates is useful for performing reconnaissance because it enables the adversary to identify the most interesting system about those that were infected and prepare the next set of malicious tools to attempt bypassing the security measures on that endpoint. In other words, if you spotted brbbot.exe being used in your environment, there is a reasonable chance that you've caught the adversary relatively early in his efforts to compromise you. In the case of brbbot.exe, we were dealing with HTTP connections, which we could examine using a network sniffer with the help of DNS and web services running on REMnux.

Summary

In this chapter, we explored and learned the concepts and tools necessary to pursue the analysis of a malicious binary on the code level. We also took a dive into the world of assembly language and debuggers by experimenting with various features offered by x64dbg. All of this proved to be helpful during the code analysis process and offered the opportunity to examine code associated with a malicious executable.

References

Afianian, A., Niksefat, S., Sadeghiyan, B., & Baptiste, D. (2020). Malware dynamic analysis evasion techniques: A survey. *ACM Computing Surveys, 52*(6), 1–28. https://doi.org/10.1145/3365001

Alaeiyan, M., Parsa, S., & Conti, M. (2019). Analysis and classification of context-based malware behavior. *Computer Communications, 136*, 76–90. https://doi.org/10.1016/j.comcom.2019.01.003

An investigation of cryptojacking: Malware analysis and defense strategies. (2019). *Journal of Strategic Innovation and Sustainability, 14*(1). https://doi.org/10.33423/jsis.v14i1.987

Coulter, R., Han, Q.-L., Pan, L., Zhang, J., & Xiang, Y. (2020). Code analysis for intelligent cyber systems: A data-driven approach. *Information Sciences, 524*, 46–58. https://doi.org/10.1016/j.ins.2020.03.036

Imran, M., Afzal, M. T., & Qadir, M. A. (2017). A comparison of feature extraction techniques for malware analysis. *Turkish Journal of Electrical Engineering and Computer Sciences, 25*(2), 1173–1183. https://doi.org/10.3906/elk-1601-189

Monnappa, K. A. (2018). *Learning malware analysis: Explore the concepts, tools, and techniques to analyze and investigate windows malware*. Packt Publishing. https://www.packtpub.com/product/learning-malware-analysis/9781788392501

Sibi Chakkaravarthy, S., Sangeetha, D., & Vaidehi, V. (2019). A survey on malware analysis and mitigation techniques. *Computer Science Review, 32*, 1–23. https://doi.org/10.1016/j.cosrev.2019.01.002

Yakura, H., Shinozaki, S., Nishimura, R., Oyama, Y., & Sakuma, J. (2019). Neural malware analysis with attention mechanism. *Computers & Security, 87*, 101592.

Printed in the United States
by Baker & Taylor Publisher Services